Wild Bill Sullivan

Wild Bill
Sullivan

•

KING OF THE
HOLLOW

By Ann Hammons

UNIVERSITY PRESS
OF MISSISSIPPI
Jackson

DEDICATED TO THE MEMORY
OF MY PARENTS
Eula Sullivan
and
Virgil Marion Howell

Library of Congress Cataloging in Publication Data
Hammons, Ann.
  Wild Bill Sullivan, king of the Hollow.
  Bibliography: p.
  1. Sullivan, William Cicero, 1851–1932.
2. Sullivan family.   3. Sullivan's Hollow, Miss.—
History.   4. Folk-lore—Mississippi—Sullivan's
Hollow.   5. Sullivan's Hollow, Miss.—Bibliography.
I. Title.
F349.S93H35   976.2'582'00992 [B]   80-19625
ISBN 0-87805-568-1 (pbk.)

CONTENTS

PREFACE

THIS IS THE STORY of Tom Sullivan, the founder of Sullivan's Hollow and the patriarch of twenty-two children; but primarily, it is the story of Tom's grandson, Wild Bill Sullivan, the undisputed "king of the Hollow." The reputation of William C. "Wild Bill" Sullivan of Sullivan's Hollow, Mississippi, is still familiar to many native Mississippians. It has long been my desire to seek the truth about Wild Bill, regardless of what the truth might reveal.

I have felt that someone should sift through the legends told about this unique character and preserve the truth for posterity. I wanted to record impressions of those who have firsthand remembrances of Wild Bill, and I realize that more and more of this generation are dying each passing year. Wild Bill was my mother's grandfather. He told his story to my father, V. M. Howell, who recorded it in a short unpublished manuscript in 1930. I have some remembrance of my great-grandfather before his death in 1932. Coupling these factors with my training as a historian, I decided to try to record an accurate picture of Wild Bill's life.

The following story is the culmination of that search. It is not the entire story. Gaps will be evident to some readers. In considering a life as colorful as that of Bill Sullivan, one finds differing versions. There will be some parts that people will disagree with because they have always heard it told differently. Then again, there will be some episodes here that have never been told in print—at least not in the detail presented here.

Naturally, the farther back into time that one is able to trace his forefathers, the more difficult it becomes to verify what few records can be found. Separating the myths from reality is a never-ending process. One should realize, however, that there is always some plausibility interwoven with the legends, or else the tall tales would never have been believed and preserved from generation to generation. Even though with repeated tellings distortions creep in, the eccentric becomes humorous, and day-by-day mundane activities become unheralded valor, much truth can still be gleaned by the careful researcher. In this publication wherever conclusions have been inferred or deduced from existing data rather than being verified from primary sources, the reader is so informed. In fact, for the years prior to 1830 I generally have presented the accumulated data and will let the reader arrive at his own conclusions.

Part 1 traces the Sullivans from Ireland to Mississippi. It also contains some characteristics of life in Sullivan's Hollow in the early nineteenth century. This section centers primarily around the origin of Thomas Sullivan and the Sullivan clan. Part 2 contains the story of the many pranks and violent episodes concerning Wild Bill. Part 3 contains other stories about Smith County, treats the changes wrought in the Hollow by the so-called progress of the twentieth century, and discusses the effects of these changes upon the unique character of the Sullivan community.

There are many people to whom I am indebted, ranging from the assistants in various archives to complete strangers who responded to my plea for help. Many friends merely listened. A few special people must be named: Aunt Dovie and Uncle Shep Sullivan (my father's sister who married my mother's brother), whose help enabled this story to be told; great-uncle Boyd Sullivan, the youngest son of Wild Bill; Uncle Milton Sullivan, who told me many stories; Mrs. Maxine Watts, an authority on the Sullivan genealogy; D. K. Sullivan, Washington County, Alabama; Chester Sullivan, who recently wrote a book entitled *Sullivan's Hollow*; Ray, my husband, Mary, my daughter, and Fannie Mae, my twin sister, who served as my readers; and lastly my father, Virgil Marion Howell who, although deceased in 1966, left the legacy of the unpublished manuscript mentioned previously.

PART ONE:
Wild Irish Roots
1775–1850

Wild Bill Sullivan and his wife Juriah Keyes (June 1930)

The Sullivan
Mystique

NOT MANY MILES from the heartland of Mississippi lies a valley of piney woods, unchanged by modern progress. Virtually ignored, except by returning kinfolk or curiosity-seekers, it is a valley dotted by well-kept farms, tended by humble but proud people who ask no more than to be left alone. The refreshing stream that winds through the hills and in and around the farms carries the name of its people.

A century and a half ago, a man came to the valley, bringing his wife and unborn son. All their worldly goods were piled high on one squeaky wagon. They dreamed of owning land in this region, filled with wild game and lush forest and inhabited only by Choctaw Indians. After staking out a claim, this pioneer family built a sturdy log cabin and settled down to carving out an existence in the wilderness. Sons and daughters, eleven in all, were born at regular intervals. As time passed, the man established another woman in a hut across the hollow from the first. Some say she was a woman he had known earlier; others say she was a Choctaw Indian maid, barely out of her teens. And she, too, bore the man eleven sons and daughters. Other kinfolk from Alabama, from Georgia, and from South Carolina heard of the valley and began to move in. As sons grew to manhood, disagreements arose, and tempers flared. The valley soon established a reputation for violence and as one ruled exclusively by and for the family members.

Fifty years went by, and another man, a grandson of the first, swaggered up and down the valley gaining a reputation as the most notorious of the clan. He killed numerous individuals—some say as

3

many as fifty, although seldom could anyone name a victim. Others said he was the meanest son-of-a-gun that ever walked the face of the earth, and that he took his grandfather's place as the self-appointed tyrant of the valley. His mother called him leadproof, the clan called him wild, and his enemies called him everything their imaginative ire could think of. He drank heavily and brawled week nights as well as on Saturdays, fouling the air with curses and drunken shouts. He feared no man, and although sought by the law for many deeds, he successfully appealed the only conviction against him. He was a notorious figure in his day.

Yet his keen sense of humor revealed itself in some of the most outlandish pranks known to man. He could never resist playing jokes on strangers and relatives alike. Salesmen went miles out of their way to avoid going through the valley for fear of being plowed all day and fed fodder at night like a mule.

However, because he was a man of his word, he earned the respect of high-ranking state officials. He died practically penniless, and having rarely traveled outside his home state. Yet newspapers proclaimed his death, and, years later, continue to print articles about him, for the myths and legends concerning this man and the mystique surrounding this valley fascinate readers today.

This man was Wild Bill Sullivan, king of the Hollow; and this is his story.

The Early
Sullivans

THE NAME SULLIVAN is derived from the Irish O'Suillobnean, meaning "one-eyed man." It is not known from which line of the family the first Sullivan immigrants to America were descended, but it is generally believed that all Sullivans are of common ancestry.

The book *South Carolinians in the Revolution* notes that the Sullivans of the United States are descended from Sir Owen O'Sullivan of Ireland who traces his ancestry back to the days of Emperor Charlemagne.[1] The general assumption is that the O'Sullivans (or Sullivans, Sullivants, Sulivents) came from Ireland. By 1300, most of these Sullivans came from the southwest counties of Cork, Kerry, and Limerick. There were many Sullivans in the colonies by the 1750s, and doubtless most of these could be traced to Ireland.[2]

Many accounts state that the Thomas Sullivan who founded Sullivan's Hollow in Mississippi was born in Ireland and that he emigrated to the New World, possibly with his brothers. Various sources have always maintained that he came to South Carolina, to Georgia, and then to a farm in Alabama before founding Sullivan's Hollow in Mississippi. A great number of Irishmen left Ireland dur-

---

[1]Sara Sullivan Ervin, *South Carolinians in the Revolution* (Baltimore: Baltimore Genealogical Publishing Co., 1965). Gilbert Doan, a noted genealogist, cautions researchers against this practice of associating common people with royalty.

[2]In Register of Deeds containing the abstracts of wills for Limerick, Ireland, November 4, 1708, there is a will for Darby Sullivan, who had four sons named John, Thomas, Daniel, and Dennis. Records also indicate that other early Sullivans were Onery (1656), Daniel (1704), and Darby (1728).

ing this period because they were Catholics being persecuted by Anglicans. However, Thomas Sullivan's ancestors seem to have been non-Catholic. Also these Sullivans, probably yeomen, were not of sufficient importance to be persecuted for political reasons.

Charleston was founded as a town in South Carolina in 1670. Sullivans were among the first fleet passengers to the city. Flor O'Sullivan was the captain of one of these ships, and Sullivan's Island which lies today in the Bay of Charleston honors him. Early records reveal that John Sullivan and Daniel Sullivan came to America in 1670; the former, along with his wife Rachael, had extensive landholdings along the Ashley River.[3] An Owen Sullivan was killed in the Revolutionary War, and an annuity was paid to his widow, Susannah, in 1785. The Sullivans of the William Dunkin Sullivan line trace their ancestry to Owen.[4]

For whatever cause, Sullivans were in South Carolina when the first census was taken in 1790, and there were two named Thomas, both of whom lived just west of Charleston in the Beaufort District, whose records burned during the Civil War. There is no Thomas Sullivan listed in the 1800 or 1810 census of South Carolina. Family legend claims that Thomas was from the area around Bishopville, but no verification of this data can be found.[5]

Some of the Sullivans in South Carolina bore names which appear consistently in the Sullivan lineage. It is true that such names as Thomas, James, William, John, Daniel, Mark, Samuel, and Stephen are so common among any family that no particular significance can be attached to their frequency. Even Cornelius and Owen are not unusual. However, these Sullivan names crop up in South Carolina, then abound in Georgia, are repeated in Alabama, and are the given names of heads of known Sullivan families in Mississippi.

Thomas Sullivan of Smith County always said Georgia was the

[3]A. S. Salley and R. N. Olsberg, *Warrants for Land in South Carolina, 1672–1711* (Columbia: University of South Carolina Press, 1973), 32. These warrants can also be found in the *Georgia Genealogical Society Quarterly*, VII, no. 1, and in the *Abstracts from the Records of the Court of Ordinary of the Province of South Carolina, 1692–1700*, as found in the *South Carolina Genealogist*. The 1790 Census for South Carolina is fairly accurate, as are the Revolutionary War Records.

[4]Milton Sullivan, *The Sullivan Family: William Dunklin Sullivan Line* (privately printed, 1961), 1.

[5]Chester Sullivan, *Sullivan's Hollow* (Jackson: University Press of Mississippi, 1978), 6.

place of his birth. The Sullivans of Georgia lived in St. Andrew and St. Paul parishes. The Georgia colony was surveyed off into eight districts called parishes, each of which was named after early Christians. Among these were St. Paul (Augusta) and St. Andrew (Darien). When the region south of the Altamaha became part of the colony in 1763, four additional parishes were created. The boundaries of these parishes ran in a northerly direction. Thus, grants made in St. Paul and St. Andrew parishes could be neighboring lands.

Even though land records may show Sullivans in different counties in different years, most of them lived out from Augusta near Sullivan's Creek; they did not change places—the counties just changed names. St. Paul's Parish had been created in 1758 from lands of the Creek cession of May 20, 1733. Richmond County was created from St. Paul's on February 5, 1777, with Columbia County cut off from it on December 10, 1790. Washington County was created in 1784 from land obtained from the Cherokees at Augusta. Realizing these facts, the records concerning Sullivan land grants are not nearly so confusing as they first seem to be.

Prior to 1790, the records show that Thomas, Owen, and Daniel received grants in St. Andrew's Parish.[6] After 1790, the Sullivans began to sell their lands.[7] One such transaction has a note attached which states that Margaret Sullivan relinquishes her dowry.[8] Thomas Sullivan of Washington County, Alabama, was married to a

[6]*Index to the Headright and Bounty Grants of Georgia, 1756–1909* (Easley, S.C.: Southern Historical Press, 1970), Platt Book G, p. 165, and Platt Book I, p. 321, Surveyor-General's Office, show Thomas as the recipient of land grants in 1766, 1771, and 1775 in St. Andrew's Parish, and as acquiring land in 1792 in Columbia County.

[7]"Camden County Deed Records," *Georgia Genealogical Magazine* (Easley, S.C.: Southern Historical Press, 1963), VII, 361. Owen and Thomas sold land in 1790 to William Kennon, and in 1793 Thomas sold land to James Espay. Researchers interested in the Sullivans of Georgia should consult *Columbia Deed Book A* (Albany, Ga.: Georgia Pioneers). Georgia Pioneers also published *Columbia County Early Court Records.* Facts are accurately assembled from other records and are valuable to researchers of the Augusta area. The 1790 census for Georgia was burned in the War of 1812 but *A Substitute for Georgia's Lost Census, 1790* has been compiled. Researchers may also want to consult *Annals of Georgia: Liberty County:* E. M. Coulter, *A List of Early Settlers of Georgia* (Athens: University of Georgia Press, 1967); Francis H. Beckemeyer (comp.), *Abstracts of Georgia Colonial Conveyances Book C-1* (Atlanta: R. J. Taylor, Jr. Foundation, 1971); and all volumes of Frances Wynd, *They Were Here* (Albany, Ga.: privately printed, 1965–).

[8]*Columbia Deed Book,* 8.

Margaret, so this appears to be a direct linkage between the Georgia and the Alabama families.

The United States initiated the Indian factory system in 1795 whereby private traders who desired to operate or travel among the Indians had to be licensed by the government. On Tuesday, October 29, 1799, Thomas Sullivan of Columbia County, Georgia, obtained a passport from the governor of Georgia to make a trip through the land of the Creeks. Thomas's passport reads: "On application from William Binion, Junr, Esquire accompanying recommendation from sundry inhabitants of Columbia County; Ordered that passports be prepared for Captain William Binion, Junr, and Mr. John Roberts, and Mr. Thomas Sullivan as linguist and pilot to them through the Creek nation unto the settlements of the Tombigby and back to this state—which were presented and signed."[9]

Sullivan's Hollow descendants believe that this Thomas was their ancestor. Thomas and Owen Sullivan of Georgia sold out their Georgia holdings and were in southwest Alabama by the 1790s (see chapter 3). The 1820 census records for Georgia list no Thomas or Owen, while the 1810 Alabama records list both names. Georgia shows a Cornelius and a Mark as late as 1820, whereas they appear first in Washington County in 1830. Furthermore, Georgia shows no Sullivan living in Columbia or Liberty County by 1840, so undoubtedly they had moved to Alabama by this time.

Thus, evidence on the early Sullivans in South Carolina is inconclusive. More definite proof exists which links the Sullivans of the St. Paul Parish, later Richmond and Columbia counties, to the same Sullivan who settled Washington County, Alabama. However, since records were burned, lost, or are nonexistent, no definite father-son relationship between the names can be established.

[9]William H. Dumont, *Passports Issued by Governors of Georgia* (Washington: National Geological Society, 1962), 503.

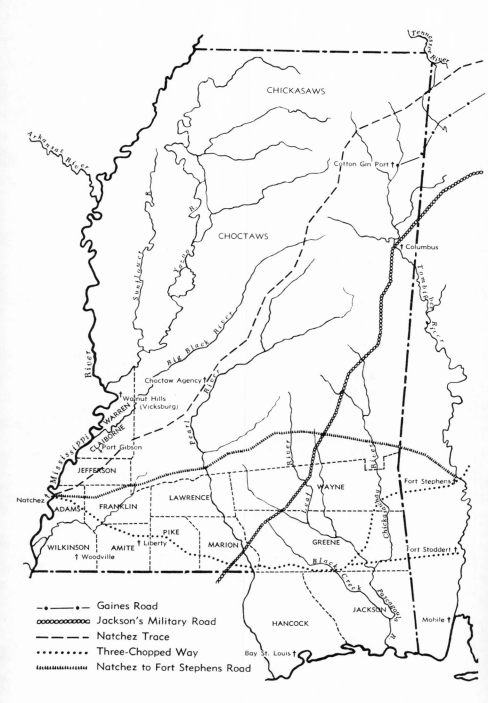

CHICKASAWS

CHOCTAWS

Arkansas River

Sunflower R.

Yazoo R.

Mississippi River

Big Black River

Pearl River

Leaf River

Chickasawhay River

Tombigbee River

Tennessee River

Black Creek

Pascagoula R.

Cotton Gin Port †

† Columbus

Choctaw Agency †

† Walnut Hills
(Vicksburg)

WARREN

CLAIBORNE

† Port Gibson

JEFFERSON

Natchez †

ADAMS

FRANKLIN

LAWRENCE

WAYNE

Fort Stephens †

WILKINSON

AMITE

PIKE

† Liberty

† Woodville

MARION

GREENE

Fort Stoddert †

JACKSON

Mobile †

HANCOCK

Bay St. Louis †

Gaines Road
Jackson's Military Road
Natchez Trace
Three-Chopped Way
Natchez to Fort Stephens Road

TERRITORIAL ROADS

The Sullivans
of Alabama

IN OCTOBER, 1799, Thomas Sullivan of Columbia County, Georgia, secured a passport to go to the Tombigbee River. Undoubtedly he went to the southwestern part of what is now Washington County, Alabama. In an 1805 treaty with the Creeks, the United States was able to establish a horsepath and to maintain it. With the Creek chiefs' consent, this horsepath became the basis of the Old Federal Road to Fort St. Stephens, but it was used by adventuresome pioneers long before it became a road or before the land was ceded by the Creeks to become part of the Mississippi Territory. The Old Federal Road crossed central Georgia from Augusta and exited that state below what is now Columbus. From there it went to Fort Mims on the Alabama River where an early ferry existed, or to Fort Stoddard on the Mobile River. The road then took the traveler to Fort St. Stephens. From this Alabama fort, the road continued west to Natchez, located on the Mississippi River. Probably this is the path that Thomas and his two Georgia neighbors took to the Tombigbee.

The Alabama and the Tombigbee join in Washington County to form the Mobile River which flows into the Gulf of Mexico at Mobile. This port city, founded as early as 1711, became British territory after the French and Indian War ended in 1763; Spain, who had previously controlled the territory, had assisted France in the war, and thus she had to forfeit it to the winner, England. McIntosh Bluff, an ancient seat of the Tohome Indians, was included in the first Choctaw Session to the British in 1765. McIntosh Bluff on the Tombigbee is the earliest American settlement north of 31° in the present state of Alabama, and was the first county seat of Washington County.

Pioneers from the southeastern seaboard were among the first to settle in this region. They came in large numbers to the Alabama and Tombigbee river valleys. After the Revolutionary War ended in 1783, planters from Georgia, Virginia, and South Carolina came with their slaves and established cotton plantations in the fertile river valleys. Some travelers used the Great Trading Path, as the Creeks called a road that transversed central Georgia over to the Tallapoosa River in Alabama. However, pioneers from Georgia and South Carolina, planning to go to the Tombigbee area, used the Old Federal Road or, as it was commonly called, the "Three Notch Road," from the triple blazes chopped on trees to mark the route. One branch of the Three Notch Road went southward from Mims Ferry across the Alabama River to Mobile; another branch extended to Natchez.

In the Treaty of Paris, 1783, which gave independence to the former English colonies and ended the Revolutionary War, the United States returned all of the territory south of the thirty-first parallel to Spain, as that country had helped the United States in the struggle for freedom. On both sides of the border were Americans who owned land. About 1772, Thomas Bassett, a British loyalist, had migrated to this area from near Augusta, Georgia, to escape persecution from American patriots. In 1776, he had received from King George III a grant of 750 acres on the west side of the Tombigbee River, where he established a plantation. About 1780, he was murdered by Indians near a creek that today bears his name. In 1785, a treaty was made with the Choctaw Nation at the Indian Congress held in Mobile that allowed settlements to be made on the western side of the Tombigbee River. In 1795, Spain ceded the entire area back to the United States, and in 1798 the U.S. government created the Mississippi Territory.

The growth of the counties made from this territory parallel the migration of the Sullivans to Alabama from Columbia County, Georgia (St. Paul's Parish). On June 4, 1800, Washington County, Alabama, was created by a proclamation of Winthrop Sargent, governor of the Mississippi Territory. It consisted of all the Mississippi Territory that lay between the Pearl River (presently in Mississippi) and the Chattahoochee River (now the Alabama-Georgia boundary). The southern boundary was the 31° north parallel (presently the Alabama-Florida boundary), and the northern boundary was a line drawn due east from the mouth of the Yazoo River, which empties into the Mississippi. This line extended eastward across Alabama to Phoenix City. Since Washington County comprised 25,000 square miles, it was later cut down to extend eastward only to the Alabama River instead of to the Chattahoochee.

In 1809, Baldwin County was created from Washington County. It is the only county in Alabama not located today where it was first established. At first, it was made from the southern part of Washington County and lay between that county and the Spanish province of West Florida. However, sometime after the admission of Alabama as a state in 1817, old Baldwin County was divided between Mobile County and Washington County. The eastern part of what was then Mobile County across Mobile Bay from the town of Mobile was made into a new county named Baldwin. Furthermore, Clarke County, which lay east of the Tombigbee River and across to the Pearl, was made from Washington on December 10, 1812. When the Mississippi–Alabama line was established in 1817, part of the territory was given to Mississippi. A census, taken by Mississippi in 1816 in connection with its movement for statehood, involved the Tombigbee areas of Clarke, Washington, Baldwin, and Monroe counties in Alabama.

It seems reasonable to assume that, when Thomas Sullivan got the passport in 1799 to guide his two neighbors in Columbia County to the Tombigbee River, it was not the first time that he had been to this area, nor was he the first Sullivan to settle there.

Early records verify that Stephen, Owen, Eugene, and Thomas were in this area prior to 1800. Stephen, who lived around Boatyard Lake and Fort Mims, countersigned with Daniel McGillivray papers in 1795 or 1796 confirming a treaty with the Indians of this area. In June, 1795, he certified that a man named James Steward had bought a horse from him and that the transaction had occurred in the Tensaw-Tombigbee river area. Stephen had reached maturity by this time.

Beginning August 7, 1805, all homesteads granted in previous years had to be registered with the U.S. Public Land Office at Fort St.

Stephens. One claim recorded that day was made by John Hinson as the administrator for Owen Sullivan, deceased, for 400 acres of land situated in Washington County on the western side of the Tombigbee River, by virtue of an order or warrant of survey from the Spanish government, dated June 10, 1795.[1] This identical claim was previously registered with the Spanish at Mobile as "Hoen Solivan." The four heirs of Owen Sullivan filed for 400 acres of land of first quality, with 40 acres of improved land thereon, at $2.50 per acre for a total of $1,000.

Spanish records list an American named Eugenio Sullivan at Fort St. Stephens also, but no further record can be found on him. Residents of the area today believe he moved west.

Owen's land grant is interesting because of the terminology used to describe its boundaries. It reads:

> Beginning on west margin of Tombigby River to the upper side of the mouth of Three R Lake, thence up the margin of said R to a sweet gum at the mouth of Barker's cutoff or Bayou to a willow on the E margin of said lake, thence down the margin of said lake 66 chains 50 links to a hickory, thence N 38° E 37 chains to a stake, thence S 64° E 76 chains to a stake, thence with the Waters of a branch of said lake to the place of beginning.[2]

On November 15, 1802, Owen D. Sullivan conveyed his right and title to sixty acres of land in Washington County to James Bilbo; again, in 1805, this James Bilbo is recorded as a neighbor of Owen's when he sold for $100 this same sixty acres bound on the upper side by lands granted to Owen "Sulavant."[3] A map of 1805 of the Tensaw region with a list of houses on the east side of the Tensaw and the west side of the Tombigbee shows house #35 as "Sylevan" and #34 as "Bilbow."[4] Tax records also show that the heirs of Owen filed for tax purposes on this same grant after their father's death. A "Mrs. Sulevant" paid taxes in Baldwin County in 1816. She could be the widow of Owen and thus the mother of the Sullivans of this area.

Thomas Sullivan purchased 190 acres of land at two dollars an

[1] U.S. Public Land Office Records, Applications for Homesteads (MT) Registration August 7, 1805–August 19, 1822, B. No. 5, registered August 14, 1805.

[2] *Ibid.*

[3] "Washington County, Alabama Earliest Deed Book," *Alabama Genealogical Register*, V(1963).

[4] This map is located in the map room of the Alabama Department of Archives and History, Montgomery, Alabama.

acre in conformity with a certificate of preemption (D No 43) dated August 7, 1805. His record reads:

Entry #31 P 12 Receivers Office, Ft. St. Stephens

December 29, 1807

Thomas Sullivan, of Washington County,

For Three hundred and eighty dollars being the amount of purchase money of one hundred ninety acres of land purchased this day in conformity to a certificate preemption marked D. No. 43, dated the 7th August 1805 as appears by the Register Return . . . $380.[5]

Fort St. Stephens and later Huntsville served as Alabama's capitals, so early records were carried to either of these places. Entry dates extending from 1807 until November 6, 1817, show Thomas Sullivan's sales transaction, the interest that accrued, and payments that were made, making a total of $469.36 ½ paid.[6]

The following land deed describes another of Thomas's transactions:

The Register and Receiver East of Pearl River to the register of the Land Office of the United States living east of Pearl River. Joseph P. Kennedy, representative of Thomas Sullivan, presented by claim in due form to two hundred forty acres of land situated in Washington County and Territory aforesaid on the west side of Tombigbee River as a preemption by virtue of occupancy, agreeable to the first section of an act of the Congress of the United States, passed on the nineteenth day of January 1808, entitled an act supplemental to an act regulating the grant of land and providing for the disposal of the lands of the United States, South of the State of Tennessee.

It is hereby certified and recorded, known that the said Register and Receiver having investigated said claim and judged that the same is supported agreeably to the requirements of said Act, and the said claimant is entitled to a right of preemption to two hundred forty acres of land to be located as follows: "beginning at a black gum on the Southeast corner, thence due West sixty chains, thence due North forty chains, thence due East sixty chains, thence due South forty chains, to the beginning.[7]

A survey was made in 1800, and one block of land is labeled "Sullivan," while another directly on the Tombigbee is labeled as "T. Sullivan." Records indicate that Owen Sullivan's land was near Bil-

---

[5]Journal A., Book 49, *Fort St. Stephens U.S. Land Records*, I (1807), 12.

[6]*Ledger, Credit System, Huntsville, East of the Pearl River, 1800–1816*, Book 192 (December 30, 1807), 31.

[7]This deed was recorded in the Land Office at St. Stephens, February 22, 1808.

bo's, as can be seen at the lower left corner of the map. Thomas's lands comprised about one-half of Sunflower Bend on the Tombigbee River. John Hinson, administrator for Owen's estate, owned the remainder. Thomas probably bought the land described above because the property in the bend was low and subject to the overflow from the river when the rains came. This condition was good for the land but was a poor spot for a home. His farms today lie in old Wakefield, which is owned by a hunting club. The land claims definitely place Thomas and Owen Sullivan in this area in the 1795–1809 period.

In 1803, two land offices were authorized by the U.S. government for the Mississippi Territory. One of these lay west of the Pearl River; and the other, east of the Pearl, was Fort St. Stephens. These offices handled the knotty problem of disposing of land with conflicting claims. Surveying the lands was slow and difficult so it was 1809 before the lands east of the Pearl River were officially opened. By this time most of the land on the Tombigbee had already been homesteaded.[8]

That the Sullivans were active in Washington County by 1809 is further verified by *The Territorial Papers of the United States*. On February 7 of that year, a petition was sent to the president and Congress by the inhabitants of said county, which read:

> ... since 3 March 1807 when the law was passed limiting immigrants to settle on publick lands, a large number of immigrants have come in ignorant of the restrictions of the law and have settled on publick lands lately ceded by Choctaw Indians to the U.S. and, are real American citizens, expected lands to be opened for sale. Petition ask that petitioners be allowed the right of preemption since to not do so would constitute an act of cruelty, and would drive the settlers to Florida ... that the free navigation of the Mobeal be secured as we have to pay a foreign sovereign for import and the same for exporting.[9]

Among the many petitioners were the names of Thomas Sullivant, Owen Sullivant, and Thomas Sullivant, Junior. These petitions confirm what John K. Bettersworth says in *Mississippi: A History*: "Actually there was plenty of land, but many of the set-

[8]John K. Bettersworth, *Mississippi: A History* (Austin: Steck Co., 1959), 142.
[9]Clarence E. Carter (comp.), *Territorial Papers 1798–1817* (New York: AMS Press, 1973), V, 693–94.

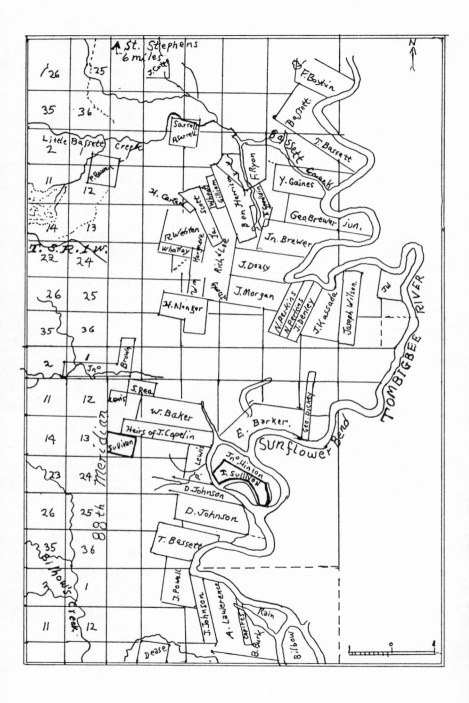

tlers had no legal claim of any sort. These squatters lost no time in demanding the right to pre-empt or claim land by prior settlement." Bettersworth notes that the law in 1803 "allowed squatters to hold by pre-emption right as much as 640 acres, with the privilege of installment payments. The first fourth of the purchase price was due in January, 1806. Under the 1803 law, some 700 squatter families were confirmed in their lands to the Natchez area, and 108 families won titles in the *Tombigbee* area to the east."[10]

The people of this area talked of separation from the Mississippi Territory as early as 1803, complaining that the Natchez area dominated the territory and that the interest of the interior section was neglected. Six years later there was a second backwoods effort to achieve separation. A long petition from the inhabitants east of the Pearl River in Mississippi Territory was sent to the speaker of the House of Representatives in May, 1809, in which they asked "for a division of the Mississippi Territory and that a new government may be erected, to be bounded on the west by Pearl River, on the east by the State of Georgia, on the north by the State of Tennessee, and on the south by the national boundary dividing the Territory from the Dominions of the King of Spain."[11] Among the signers of this petition was Owen Sullivant. In December, 1809, an additional memorial to the petition contained the signature of Thomas Sullivant, as well as that of James Bilbo, Sr. This petition supports the idea that discontent was rife in the eastern area of the Pearl and Tombigbee river sections. The products they bought had to come down the Mississippi, and then up through the Spanish fort of Mobile where a toll was collected. By the time a barrel of flour costing four dollars in Natchez got to the eastern backwoods of the Tombigbee area, it cost sixteen dollars.[12] It is little wonder that these Sullivans and others were unhappy with this arrangement.

The territorial papers show the petition was first tabled, then sent to a committee. The dispute was not settled until March, 1817, when the present line dividing Alabama and Mississippi was established by the United States in preparation for Mississippi to become a state in December. Alabama remained a territory until 1819.

[10]Bettersworth, *Mississippi*, 141–42.
[11]Carter, *Territorial Papers*, 732–37.
[12]Bettersworth, *Mississippi*, 129.

Examination of census records reveals added information about Thomas and Owen Sullivan. Baldwin County having been made from southern Washington County in 1809, the census for Washington County, 1810, shows a Daniel Sullivan, while the census of Baldwin County, 1810, lists a Thomas Sullivan with seven whites. Again, in 1820, Thomas is listed with a total of twelve in his household. Thomas died in 1820 and is buried in a cemetery near old Wakefield. This Alabama Thomas Sullivan must be the father of the Mississippi Thomas, who must be the Thomas Jr. mentioned in the petition of 1809. Thomas Sullivan, Jr. appears on the real and personal tax rolls of Washington County, 1805. Thomas Jr. also filed for a preemption claim at Fort St. Stephens August 7, 1805, with another entry recording a transfer of property on June 16, 1806. On March 21, 1807, Peace Seth transferred land to Thomas Sullivan, Jr.

Living in this same county in 1830 were Owen (40–50 years old), Cornelius (30–40 years old), Stephen (30–40 years old), and Mark (20–30 years old), evidently brothers. Perhaps all four, along with Thomas, who had migrated to Mississippi by this time, descended from the Owen who received the original Spanish grant in 1795. Family legend persists that Owen moved to Mississippi and never returned to Alabama. However, he never appears on any early records of Mississippi. One informant surmises that he moved on out west, possibly to Texas.

D. K. Sullivan (born 1908), a resident of Wagarville, Washington County, Alabama, sheds some light on these Sullivans in Alabama.[13] He says that, although he cannot prove it, he feels sure that Thomas Sullivan was the father of Mark, and that the Owen with the Spanish claim of 1795 was the father of Cornelius. This would make Mark a brother to the Thomas who moved to Sullivan's Hollow.

Mark appears on the special tax/census rolls of Simpson County, Mississippi, in 1824, but nothing appears about him in Mississippi records again. He must have returned to Alabama and is the Mark of the 1830 census. On October 28, 1829, he married Jemimah Teddler of Mobile County. Records also show that Mark was on the census rolls of 1850 in Greensboro, Alabama. This was the site of the state

[13]Interview, D. K. Sullivan, Wagarsville, Ala., 1978.

prison where Mark was serving a term for killing a Mr. Jordan whose son in turn killed Mark before the time of the 1860 census. Mark and some of his family are believed buried near the old Sullivan property in Washington County, Alabama, but no one is allowed on the grounds today to verify the unmarked sites.

Cornelius's first wife was Mary Basset, whom he married about 1815 and who died before the 1830 census. On March 31, 1831, Cornelius married Rachel Danley, born in 1811. They had two sons born in Alabama before moving to Mississippi prior to 1840. Since his older children, even those by his first wife, probably went to Mississippi with him, this provides a plausible answer to the question about the origin of the Sullivans that married Mississippi Sullivans.

Cornelius's children, Solomon (b. 1838), Elizabeth (b. 1844), and George W. (b. July 4, 1846, father to D. K. Sullivan's mother), were born in Mississippi. D. K. says that he can remember his grandfather's talking about the Mississippi kinfolk who would come back to the Tombigbee area to visit the Sullivans. It is also known that James, the oldest son of Thomas of Sullivan's Hollow, went back to this area to get his second wife, Patsy Rollins. In 1849, Cornelius and his family moved back to Alabama near Bassett Creek where another son, Christopher Columbus, was born in 1852.

Oral history always maintained that Stephen was killed at Sunflower in 1850 and left all his property to his son, James Johnson Sullivan. Stephen's descendants appear in the area census as late as 1860; some moved to Jackson, Alabama, and their descendants live there today. These Sullivans in Alabama, therefore, seem directly related to the Sullivans of Smith County, Mississippi.

Thomas Sullivan's house. It was built sometime between 1810 and 1820 and is the oldest house in Sullivan's Hollow.

Thomas Sullivan
of Sullivan's Hollow

THOMAS SULLIVAN, the founder of Sullivan's Hollow and the ancestor of thousands of Sullivans now living, was born in Georgia. His family originally came to Georgia from South Carolina. During colonial days, the Sullivans lived in the area west of Augusta (St. Paul's Parish) that became Columbia County, Georgia. As many as nine Sullivan families lived in this area during 1750 to 1800. Among those mentioned frequently in surviving records are Thomas, Cornelius, Owen, William, John, Daniel, Stephen, Samuel, and Mark.

At some time between 1795 and 1810 the Sullivans moved from Georgia to present-day Washington County, Alabama. Living in this area before 1800 were Owen, Eugene, Thomas, and Stephen. Owen died before 1805, and Thomas by 1821; by 1830, four Sullivan families were headed by Cornelius, Owen, Mark, and Stephen.

Thomas Sullivan, Jr. was in Alabama by 1807 and in Mississippi possibly as early as 1810. Many Arnolds lived in Washington County, and very likely Thomas's first wife, Elizabeth Arnold, was from this area and went with him to Mississippi. Thomas's second wife, Mary Workman, always gave Georgia as her birthplace, and there were Workmans in Columbia and Richmond counties of Georgia.

Grover Bishop interviewed many of the Sullivans living in Smith County, 1936–1938, for the 1938 Works Progress Administration. Bishop reported that Thomas was born in Bishopville, South

Carolina, in 1775.[1] Although early South Carolina records do not show any Sullivan living in this vicinity, Bishop's naming it as Thomas's birthplace indicates that it may have played a part at some time in Thomas's history, if not directly in his personal life.

Newspaper articles written since 1900 say Thomas was born in Georgia. Unfortunately, Georgia is one of those states whose records prior to 1810 were burned in the War of 1812. The United States required one's birthplace to be listed in the census records of 1840 and 1850. Thomas, living in Mississippi then, consistently listed his birthplace as Georgia. His older children, likewise, listed his birthplace as Georgia. However, some of his younger sons in the 1870, 1880, and 1900 censuses listed their father's birthplace variously as Mississippi, or Georgia, or South Carolina. Since most of these children, like their parents, could neither read nor write, and since Thomas had died in 1855, it is more likely that the older children knew their father's actual birthplace. There is little reason to suspect that he was foreign born. None of Thomas's children ever listed Ireland as his birthplace so it is safe to assume that he was a native American. V. M. Howell in a manuscript entitled *Authentic History of Sullivan's Hollow,* says, "to state that he came from Scotland, Ireland, England, or any other country would be a guess, because none of them ever remember hearing their grandfather Thomas as saying from what country he came."[2]

Yet the Irish origin persists. Ray Thompson, author of a column "Know your Coast" published in such papers as the *Gulfport-Herald,* reports the family legend that Thomas was one of nine Irish brothers who came from the South Carolina mountains.[3] Howell also states that Thomas came from the hills of South Carolina. Thus through oral tradition, the legend has been perpetuated.

In fact, speculation also persisted about the date of Thomas's birth. The tombstone erected at his grave in the Alex Sullivan cemetery in Smith County, Mississippi, gives his birthdate as January 15, 1775, and his death as June 10, 1855. Two things about

[1] Grover Bishop, "A History of Sullivan's Hollow" (unpublished manuscript, 1938, Mississippi Department of Archives and History), 1

[2] Virgil M. Howell, "Authentic History of Sullivan's Hollow" (unpublished manuscript, 1939, in possession of his daughter Ann Hammons, Tifton, Georgia), 1.

[3] Ray M. Thompson, "Mississippi's Famous Feuding Sullivans," *Gulfport-Biloxi Herald,* June 3, 1959.

his birthdate are troublesome. First, for the 1840 and the 1850 census he stated that he was born in 1785. Second, if born in 1775, he would have been thirty-five when his oldest child, James, was born, an almost incredible fact, since he subsequently fathered twenty-one children.

This Thomas Sullivan is not the one listed in the Amite or in the Jefferson County census. Thomas Sullivan of Smith County is not listed in any of the early censuses of Mississippi since he lived in lands belonging to the Choctaws and since the United States did not list whites living in the Choctaw Nation. Most of what was then Simpson County was granted in the Second Choctaw Cession of 1820, and this part of Simpson County included part of what is now the western area of Smith County where Thomas Sullivan lived. Thus, in a special census of births in Simpson County in 1823–1824, Thomas Sullivan is listed as having had a son born that year, as is Mary Workman, who later became his second wife. Smith County territory was obtained mainly from the Third Choctaw County Cession of 1830, and so Thomas appears in the U.S. censuses of 1840 and 1850 as well as on Smith County Real and Personal Tax Rolls of the 1830s and the 1840s.

But Thomas Sullivan did settle in Mississippi about 1810 and gave his name to the Hollow. He spent some time around Jaynesville, Mississippi, in the southeastern part of Simpson County before arriving at his future home two and one-half miles south of Mize. Howell's manuscript describes Sullivan's move to Smith County:

> Thomas and his wife, traveling in an ox wagon, stopped on the Big Buoy River [located south of present day Sullivan's Hollow in Covington County], cleared a patch of land, erected a small log house, and raised corn, tobacco, and vegetables. Their chief support was drawn from the woods and streams by hunting and fishing. Game such as deer, turkey, bear, and smaller game were found in abundance around their settlement. A traveler one day chanced into the settlement. He told them of the splendid country up in Smith County, where game of every kind was very plentiful, and which had good fishing waters, rich fertile soil, with very few people living there. Thomas and his wife decided to pack up their few belongings, leave their Buoy home, and journey to Smith County. If they liked the country, they would stay; otherwise, they would return to Buoy. Of course, they never returned.[4]

[4]Howell, "Authentic History," 1.

Thomas was a rough, burly pioneer, typical of the men who settled America. He had a hot temper and was strong enough to crush a bear. While living in Alabama, Tom had gotten into a fight with another Alabama giant, and a titanic struggle ensued that lasted an entire day. When Tom and his mighty adversary could not finish each other off with blows and strangleholds, they took to chewing each other. It is said that when Tom finally dragged himself home, his woman had to pick the other fella's flesh from his teeth, he had chewed him so badly.

After Tom moved to Mississippi, his reputation as a fighter continued. It is said that he could whip any three men at the same time. Even when Tom was an old man, he used to pick fights just for the exercise. Tom's arrogance grew with his prosperity, and many of his neighbors moved away, either from fear or hatred. Many of these stories have been exaggerated, no doubt, and many may be wholly fabricated.

Thus throughout the 160 years of its existence, Sullivan's Hollow has been a favorite topic for magazine stories. *Life* magazine featured an article, "Sullivan Hollow, Meanest Valley in America," in which the author classified Thomas as being close-lipped, though an excellent farmer. The article further stated that Thomas had "passed on his secretiveness and vindictiveness to his descendants, and now when cars groan through the valley's narrow, rutted roads, little old ladies peer suspiciously from behind gingham curtains; outsiders are barely tolerated, and when the men of Sullivan's Hollow talk about their relatives, they keep glancing over their shoulders."[5]

In his time, Tom Sullivan was supposed to have engaged in many fighting scrapes. Mac Sullivan, a grandson of Thomas, once told Grover Bishop that Thomas was the champion bare-fist fighter in the Hollow. Furthermore, he would take his sons to old Westville in Simpson County and let them fight all who dared to challenge them. The custom was for two men to hold a rope taut between the two fighters. Sometimes the fighters would battle each other for hours, but when one of them wanted to quit, he would holler "Nuff." The two fighters would go get a drink while another of his sons would

[5]William Sartor, "Sullivan's Hollow: Meanest Valley in America," *Life*, October 2, 1967, p. 10.

take on another fighter. This kind of entertainment would go on for a week or so, with Thomas intervening if it appeared that either of the fighters was going to be seriously hurt.

Stories say that Thomas Sullivan had extensive landholdings in Smith County, and that as his children married, he gave each of them 160 acres. Much of his land probably had accrued to him under squatter's rights. As long as he homesteaded land that was officially Indian territory, no one questioned his claims. But by 1835 when Sullivan's lands were formally made a part of the newly formed Smith County, he had to declare the purchase of the land and commence to pay taxes on them. Tax records indicate that he owned no more than a couple of hundred acres and that his personal property was of a minor nature. At one time he is listed as owning three slaves. Like most residents of the area, the Sullivans seemed to favor cattle raising more than crops for cash income. However, hogs and cattle roamed the woodlands rather than being raised in lush pastures. The annual roundup and separation of the cattle by families, and the journey to Natchez or Mobile to sell the animals and purchase necessities were the highlights of the year.

In 1855, Thomas died as he lived, fighting in a horrible manner. His pain was so severe that he refused to allow anyone to touch him. Before death, he seemed to be in a trance, complaining of darkness though in broad daylight. Although widely known for his violence and as a man to be greatly feared, he was nevertheless respected by the many people who lived in or near Sullivan's Hollow.

To the right of his grave lies his first wife, Elizabeth Arnold, and to the left lies his second wife, Mary Workman. Elizabeth's parentage is practically unknown, although there were Arnolds who lived not far from the Sullivans in Alabama. Accounts about Mary are so varied as to be highly speculative. What seems to be the simple truth is that he fathered children by both wives, probably eight sons and three daughters by Elizabeth, and eight sons and three daughters by Mary.[6] In some stories, Mary is a former maid to the Sullivans who came with them from Ireland; in others, she is a young and beautiful

---

[6]Although room for variance exists, the author believes that his children by Elizabeth Arnold were James, Margaret, Thomas, Loderick, Stephen, Owen, Joseph, Dan, Celia, Fredrick, and Clara, and that his children by Mary Workman were Thomas Jefferson, Caroline, Henderson, Eliza Jane, Mark, Wiley, Mary Ann, Samuel R., Cornelius, Loughton, and Alexander.

Indian maiden who came to the Hollow with her mother and who became such a favorite of bearded Tom that he let her carry the key to the smokehouse. Other legends say that Mary was brought by Tom to the Hollow after her mother died in Natchez. Common consensus has always been that Mary did live in the Hollow before the first Mrs. Sullivan died, and that Tom married her after his first wife's death. Mary lived until 1891, thirty-six years after her husband died, so more people in the 1900s remembered her, while none of today's inhabitants knew Thomas personally. After Thomas's death, their son, Conn, moved into the log house with his mother. Conn's wife died November 2, 1882, and Mary did the housework for Conn and his children. Mary was totally blind by the time of her death at age eighty-eight.

Detail of the v-notch logs used in the Sullivan home.

Early Life
in Sullivan's Hollow

IF A LINE WERE DRAWN through the center of the state of Mississippi, north to south, and another line were drawn east to west, and if a pin were inserted just southeast of where these line crossed, it would rest in the heart of Smith County. South of Smith County lies land which once was part of Spanish territory in colonial days. The county itself was founded on December 2, 1833, from land ceded by the Choctaw Indians in the Treaty of Dancing Rabbit Creek in 1830. Prior to being turned over to the United States in 1781, the land was designated as MT (Mississippi Territory) and controlled by the state of Georgia. Numerous rivers and creeks criss-cross its sandy soil. The Leaf and Chickasawhay form the Pascagoula River that empties into Pascagoula Bay. The Pearl River, with its tributaries the Strong and the Bogue Chitto, empties into the Gulf of Mexico.

The piney woods of Mississippi, originally inhabited by the Choctaw Indians, was ceded to the United States by a series of treaties beginning with the Treaty of Mount Dexter in 1805. In the great migration after the War of 1812, settlers began coming in by horseback, on foot, by wagon teams, moving west across the Fort Stephens–Natchez road and the Three Chopped Way and down Jackson's Military Road. They came by flatboats down the rivers, and later by steamboat up the Pearl. They came from the Carolinas, Georgia, and Tennessee to the land described by J. F. H. Claiborne in 1840 as "covered exclusively with the long-leaf pine; not broken, but rolling like the waves in the middle of the great ocean. The grass grows three feet high and hill and valley are studded all over with flowers of every hue."[1]

Sullivan's Hollow in the piney woods lies between the Okatoma (shining water) Creek and Cohay Creek, both of which flow south-easterly into the Leaf River. The Hollow lies south of Mize in a system of hills drained by Sullivan's Hollow Creek from its headwaters near Thomas Sullivan's house to where it joins Bunker Hill Mill Creek. Mississippi became a state in 1817, and until 1833 Simpson County comprised some of the land which in that year became part of Smith County.

Smith County was named for Captain David Smith of Hinds County. The original county seat was at Fairchild, four miles south of the present seat of Raleigh, named for Sir Walter Raleigh. In early days, the only railroad in the area was the Gulf and Ship Island Railroad, which cut across the southern part of the county, with stations at Taylorsville, Mize, Wisner, Cooley, Abel, Saratoga, and Low. Two of the oldest towns in Smith County were Polkville and Trenton, both of which were established in the 1840s. Other early rural settlements were Boykins, Lorena, Lemon, and Sylvarena.

The land to which the Sullivans came was densely forested with timber of all types. Although originally the land had been part of Georgia, treaties had opened the way for white settlers. In a little book called *Mississippi Piney Woods* (1976), Patti Carr Black describes the area:

> The southeastern quarter of Mississippi, known as the Piney Woods, extends southward from Interstate 20 to within twenty miles of the Gulf Coast, and from the Alabama line to the Brown Loam Belt west of the Pearl River. It is a high rolling land, once covered by dense stands of longleaf pine, and patches of hardwoods in the bottoms. Originally the Hollow was six miles long and three miles wide, running in a northerly crescent from west to east. But, as its reputation spread south and west and as the number of Sullivans dramatically increased, the Hollow expanded until it encompassed the southwest corner of Smith County and parts of Covington and Simpson Counties.[2]

Sullivan's Hollow (89° 34′ west longitude and 35° 46′ north latitude) is situated just off Highway 35, three miles south of Mize,

[1]Sullivan, *Sullivan's Hollow*, 8.
[2]Patti Carr Black, *Mississippi Piney Woods* (Jackson: Mississippi Department of Archives and History, 1976), 3.

Mississippi. Sullivan's Hollow encompases Section 19 Range 15W and Section 24 Range 16W, and adjacent lands along Sullivan's Hollow Creek. On the west side of the Hollow and almost midway on the line that divides the two sections north and south, Thomas Sullivan built his home, a typical pioneer cabin. Records of many early deeds for Smith County were destroyed when the courthouse burned in 1882. Among the existing records, however, are copies of two certificates of patent issued to Thomas Sullivan: Number 2161 for 73.15 acres described as the W^{2}NE^4, and Number 2162 for 36.57 acres, NE^{4}NW^4, both in Section 18, Township 10N, Range 15W. Thomas paid $1.25 per acre for this land.[3]

"The old house," "the log house," "the original house," or "Tom Sullivan's house" are terms used to describe this landmark home, which is said to be the oldest home now extant in the piney woods section of Mississippi. Thomas Sullivan reportedly built the first part of it between 1810 and 1820, and its other sections were added by Sullivan descendants in succeeding years. Only Sullivan descendants have ever occupied the house. Shep and Dovie Sullivan, who live there today, are both descendants of Thomas Sullivan.

The house is a typical example of how pioneers built homes in the 1800s. Although slight changes and improvements have been made for the comfort of the occupants, much of the handiwork is exactly as it was when the house was erected. This one-room cabin served as kitchen and bedroom for a man, his wife, and his twenty-two children.

Today, the house has five rooms, a bathroom, and other modern conveniences. The original house is the right wing, or west-end room of the home. This room probably was a few feet wider when it was originally built. The inside dimensions are sixteen feet by eighteen feet today, but the overhand roof beams reveal that at one time the room was probably twenty-two or twenty-four feet wide. It was probably shortened at the time the second pen or room was added, about seventy-five years after its original construction. Joining the two pens is the central dog trot hallway. Just below the hallway roofline is one of the old timbers that held the porch roof.

The logs in the original home were hewn with only an axe and an

---

[3] *Real and Property Tax Records* (Jackson: Mississippi Department of Archives and History).

adze. The room is nine feet two inches high, with eleven logs, varying from ten to eleven inches in width, between the sill and the ceiling. The ends of the logs are joined in the V-notch pattern and were assembled without nails. The second pen uses a modified half-dovetail notch. Although it was probably constructed by succeeding occupants, the house today has sawn planks to ceil the interior of the original pen. The two rooms are joined with a hall six feet wide, which at the rear or south end expands into an east-west arm, giving the hall a T-shaped construction, with the west arm leading to a kitchen. This kitchen adjoins the entire south side of the original room and has plumbing, modern appliances, and gas heat.

The east arm of the hall leads to the bathroom and a utility room. Chairs with cowhide bottoms flank the central hallway which contains a freezer. At the rear of the hall is a round table built in the 1930s by V. M. Howell and used by his family until about 1945 when it was passed to his sister Dovie. Mounted on an old T-model wheel, the center of the table turns. Tables such as this one were in common use around the turn of the century but are not commonly used today. Bishop reported that in 1936 the only one in use in Smith County was owned by Guff Ainsworth. Many a child has delighted in turning the table just after a visitor has spooned vegetables from the bowl, leaving the guest with only the spoon in his hand.

After Thomas Sullivan died in 1855, his second wife, Mary, continued to live there with her son, Conn Sullivan, and his family. The third occupants were Robert and Anna (Sullivan) Russell. She was the ninth child of Alexander Sullivan, the youngest of Thomas's twenty-two children. It is thought that either Robert or Conn added the second pen, the porches, and the kitchen. Robert Russell passed the house to his brother-in-law Volney Keyes, husband of Ester Ellen Sullivan. Keyes sold the house in 1921 to Virgil Marion Howell, grandson of Francis Marion Howell, who was the husband of Thomas's granddaughter, Mary Jane. Virgil married Eula Sullivan, whose grandfather was Wild Bill Sullivan, a son of Henderson (fourteenth child of Thomas) and Leah Howell Sullivan. During Virgil's brief residency in the house, Ann Hammons and her twin sister, Fannie Mae Howell Smith, were born in 1922. In 1923 Virgil gave up farming to become a railroad telegraph operator, and the present occupants, Shep and Dovie (Virgil's sister and Eula's brother), moved

into the old home place. It has been their home for over fifty years.
Shep's oldest son, Paul Sullivan, owns the home today.

John K. Bettersworth's description of backwoods living typifies
just such a house in the 1800s when Sullivans first inhabited the
valley.

The house may be a two-room frame cabin, but most probably an in-
crease in family size will have caused it to be expanded into a four-or-five
room construction with a porch across front and rear, a chimney on each
side, and the dogtrot enclosed. It sits facing the road from the edge of a
field that stretches and rolls until the lineated shade of a dark, warm
forest joins it abruptly to the sky. To the rear and to one side is the garden.
If the children are home, the front yard, creeping unsodden from beneath
the porch, is naked and clean. If the children are grown and have moved to
places of their own, verbena, old maids, phlox, and four-o'clocks crowd
each other for space. This is due more to a taste for cleanliness than for
beauty. Our housewives haven't the time to be always sweeping the yard,
so they just plant flowers and "let 'em have it". . . .

The housewife is not too busy . . . to accompany the family to town on
Saturday, and there walk about, looking at the shop windows and greeting
friends; or to prepare a shoe box of food to be auctioned to the highest
bidder at the box supper given at the church to raise money for a new
piano; or to run up to a neighbor's house, where a group of womenfolks
are "quilting a piece for Sara Adams," who is to be married just as soon as
crops are gathered and John has the time to tend to such a thing.

The "to-do" will probably be a neighborhood party—an in-gathering of
families from down the road, from over the bottom, from just across the
field a piece. It is purely social, with no labor, no "pounding presents"
attached. Death and distance are the party's only limitations. At dark the
families, from Grandpa down, begin to arrive on trucks, in wagons, in
cars, on horseback, and on foot. Two hours after dark 50 or more men,
women, young folks, and children are mingling in about the house. Warm
cordiality and equal acceptance set the tone. The old folks gravitate to the
porch and to the yard, talking crops and politics, or ;snatching a wink or
two of sleep . . . .

The young folks move restlessly in and out of the "front room" which
contains a piano or a foot-pumped organ, the storekeeper's calendar, and
the biggest feather bed and prettiest hand-tufted bedspread in the house.
Here we were direct and natural in our association, with none of the
legendary timidity in our manner. We sit on the bed, on the cane-bottom
chairs, in the windows . . . .

The water bucket, sitting on a back-porch shelf with its bright metal
dipper beside it, is popular and the boys take turns at the nearby well
bringing up bucketfulls fresh from the earth. Fried chicken, boiled ham,
banana cake, and ho'made pickles are waiting in the kitchen. Shortly

after midnight the guests begin to leave, going by families according to the distance they have to travel and their mode of getting there. By three o'clock they are gone.

There was a time in the past when our social life was tied up with work, such as house-raising, logrolling, and hog-killing. But today we have more time and economy, and our socials move on larger planes. We hold county fairs and attend barbecues, all-day singings, and religious services. There are, in turn, manifestations of the soil, of politics, and of religion and being for us.[4]

Life in early Mississippi was hard, but it was a good and satisfying life. Life moved at a slow, leisurely pace, not so much the hurrying-scurrying of today. Sometimes outsiders claimed that Sullivan women were suspicious and never let anyone inside until they had first peered to see who knocked at the door. This habit was not so much suspicion as it was a necessity for self-preservation. Sullivans always did respect the privacy of others. And, in return, they expected the neighbors and the stranger alike to respect their privacy. Like frontier women everywhere, Sullivan women shared their food, their homes, their hospitality with those who came into the Hollow for whatever reason. But there were certain things they could not stand—a lying tongue, deceitful words, and most of all, slovenliness or in their terminology, "plain sorriness." Traits such as drinking and wife-beating that would be condemned in other areas were accepted with stoicism, but a person lacking in pride and industriousness, regardless of his economic plight, was a person to be avoided.

There also was fun in the Hollow at quilting parties, when all the women gathered to quilt and visit. A woman spent the long winter evenings cutting and sewing scraps of clothes into designs for quilt tops. Homemade patterns were swapped and used over and over again. A woman's worth was determined by the caliber of her tiny even rows of stitches. Her husband made the quilting frame, to which the quilt top, inside batting, and bottom were laced. As the women quilted from the four outside edges, the quilted area was rolled up on the frames, allowing the women to reach the center portions of the quilt. Quilting parties not only provided bedding for the cold of the winters but also became the chief social events of the

---

[4]Bettersworth, *Mississippi*, 20–21.

year; these were the events at which a woman learned of the latest fashions, gossiped, and exchanged recipes. Furthermore, such gatherings provided young mothers with their only education in maternity and child rearing.

Barn-raising proved almost as popular an occasion as the quilting bee. Reserved usually for a newlywed couple, or a newly arrived family, the barn-raising was also a social outlet for country people. All the families from miles around came in their wagons on a clear sunny day to build a barn or a house for the needy or the newcomer. Hams, turkey, chicken, and all sorts of jam, jellies, and canned produce formed the menu for the day. The men worked until noon, and came in sweaty, bragging, sometimes loud, jostling each other. They wasted little time at the front porch wash-basin or waterbucket, being too eager to get at the hot fragrant food, topped off by berry pie, perhaps some buttermilk fresh from the spring, and hot cornpone.

Men ate at the first table; small boys who had spent the morning arguing over marbles, wrestling, or playing leapfrog, and little girls, dusty from playing ring-around-the-rosy or London bridge, appeared as if from nowhere and filled in the remaining places around the table. The women ate last; even they wanted it this way. After a short rest, the men returned to the work of raising the barn, knowing that as soon as dark descended, the chairs in the larger room would be pushed against the wall, a fiddle would appear, and an old-fashioned hoedown would last until the midnight hour approached.

Another interesting tradition was a ritual known as the chivaree. Young couples went through all the prenuptial teasing, gift giving, and preparation that weddings have always evoked. Usually the bridegroom had erected a two-room cabin for their first home down on the back forty a short distance away from his parents' house. About two hours after dark, the newly married couple would be awakened by the loudest noises imaginable—kitchen pans being beat upon by spoons, dishpans being pounded, bells ringing, folks yelling, hollering, and singing. This confusion would not abate until the young bride and bridegroom threw back the shutters and appeared at the window. Then cheers replaced the noise, and among the men could be heard a few ribald but good-natured remarks; the jug would surely be passed around. Only then could the young couple retire to bed again.

At first, the valley had no churches nor cemeteries. The cemeteries gradually appeared, as every few miles a space was set aside for burials. Almost every family lost a baby.

Today, people of all ages and walks of life continue to be fascinated by life in Sullivan's Hollow. Mrs. Shep Sullivan says that many who are curious about the lore of the valley stop to see the old house. She is a very gracious hostess who can tell about the olden days more capably than anyone else living today, for she was born there and has never left the Hollow except to attend Copiah-Lincoln Junior College at Wesson or to visit some of her many relatives. She is a veritable walking encyclopedia on the Sullivans. Although she will tease and say she can't see why anyone would want to see such an old place, her pride, love, and heritage are revealed in her every word. The annual reunion of the Sullivan clan has been held on the fourth Sunday in September since World War II, and the Sullivans in the old house have many visitors on that day.

Sullivan's Hollow long has been characterized as a place of violence. Various accounts state that "Sullivans are the most rip-snortin, whiskey-drinking, pistol-packin, hard-working, ornery, money-saving, go-to-church people in the world," and that "the reign of terror, of fighting, and feuding, made the Sullivans the most legendary family in Mississippi." It has also been said that "on Saturday it was customary for Sullivan menfolk to gather at one of the places, and then stand around and drink, and spit, and insult one another until the fight started. You can't go long in the Deep South before you hear of the Sullivans of Sullivan's Hollow—terrible tales of Sullivans murdering Sullivans, of fighting and feuding, of ambushes and revenge for deeds done a generation ago. Sullivan's Hollow is a common synonym for general lawlessness, covering everything from murder to moonshine and resisting arrest."[5] However, Mrs. Maxine Watts reports that most of the stories of fights, duels, and ambushes are colorful elaborations based on less interesting facts.

It has always been typical of pioneer communities to take a dim view of the time and patience required to get matters adjusted by law; hence, often the pioneers took matters into their own hands. This was true in the

[5]Harry Henderson and Sam Shaw, "The Sullivans of Sullivan's Hollow," *Colliers,* March 17, 1945, pp. 21, 82.

case of the Sullivans because there were so many of them that their disagreements tended to be all within the family. There is no reason to say
the Sullivans caused any more trouble than any other people, but because
there were so many of them, their names did occur more often than most
others. This accounts for much of the legend of "Sullivan's Hollow."[6]

Among the legends it has been said that all the clan were blue-
eyed, that they smiled when they were angry and laughed when they
fought. When they went gunning for enemy, they usually sent the
ominous warning "I reckon I got to shoot your eyes out when I see
you," and generally that is what happened.[7] One Sullivan said that
because there were so many Sullivans, every time there was a shooting or trouble one was bound to be mixed up in it, either shooting or
shot, and everyone else said, "Oh them Sullivans up in Sullivan's
Hollow are at it again."[8]

Because the valley was populated with Sullivans who chose to
keep it for the Sullivans and because Sullivans drank and had violent
tempers, the Sullivans were known for feuding with Sullivans. All of
the original participants in the actual feuds have died, and time has
dimmed the memories of those who remain. The Sullivans could
not or did not keep written records on such activities, so no one
really knows how the family feuds began. More than likely they
resulted from the same causes that have originated most feuds in
history—women, land, moonshine, misunderstandings, or gossip.
The Sullivans provided their own justice in their frontier, preferring
to settle disputes among themselves rather than waiting on or trust-
ing the law to do so.

Tales abound that people in the Hollow always wore a pistol or
carried a rifle and used it at will. Rifles were used mainly for hunting
wild game, but since a man used it for that purpose on his way to and
from a place, he carried his rifle with him most of the time. Pistols
were a different story. They were often tucked into a man's belt.
Gunbelts as used in the West were not commonly used in Smith
County. Pistols were intended to be used against people, or for quick
killings of such dangers as rattlesnakes. Wild Bill was a good shot

[6]"Sullivan's Hollow to Echo with Political Oratory," *Jackson Daily News*, July 17,
1963.
[7]Thompson, "Mississippi's Famous Feuding Sullivans."
[8]Henderson and Shaw, "Sullivans of Sullivan's Hollow," 83.

with a pistol, probably the best in the Hollow. However, even as notorious as he was with a gun, episodes show him using his fists, his knife, or his rifle more often than a pistol.

Frontier history depicts men as pulling pistols and blazing away at one another because of cheating at cards, personal insults, and name-calling, and these types of gun fights did occur in Sullivan's Hollow. However, challenging another man merely to establish one's reputation as the fastest draw did not seem to exist. Wild Bill reigned as king of the Hollow for years. Yet at no time did he engage in incidents in which he and some younger man shot it out in the streets merely for the title. This type of violence probably is greatly exaggerated in movies about the nineteenth century, and it apparently did not exist in the violence occurring in Smith County.

A person who has never lived in Sullivan's Hollow usually has a very poor conception of its people. And, unfortunately, sometimes the person that knows the least talks the most. On one occasion, a resident of the Hollow was far from home and happened to hear two preachers talking about Sullivan's Hollow. Neither of the ministers knew that the one listening in on the conversation was born and reared in Sullivan's Hollow. Their conversation ran like this:

"Were you ever in Sullivan's Hollow?"

"No."

"Well, they are the darndest illiterate, ignorant backwoodiest, bunch of people in the world."

"Yes? What about them?"

"Once, one of them strayed over to Laurel in July when ice-making first started in hot weather and visited the ice plant and saw them making ice. He went back home and told it. They had a jail over in Sullivan's Hollow and they slammed him in it. They had a preacher in the Hollow who said he was curious to know if it was true, so he went to see for himself. He went back to the Hollow and told it was true that people in Laurel were making ice in July. They slammed the Son-of-a-Gun in jail and took his right to preach away from him for twelve months. So Wild Bill selected a committee to go find out for sure. They also found it to be true, and to convince the people, Bill brought back three one-hundred-pound blocks and carried them to the Hollow. They ganged around the ice, they would pick on it, they would feel of it, they would taste of it. Finally they decided that it was ice and turned the other men out of jail."

The Sullivan Hollow native never made himself known to the two preachers.[9]

Or consider the article written in 1903 about two geologists who were coming to Smith County to look for lead deposits. The reporter could not refrain from adding that one or both of these geologists might be mistaken for revenue agents and worked to a plow for a day or two, or they might run into a feud and catch the bullets which always hit the innocent bystander.[10]

It is from such sources of information that people have gotten the impression that the people of Sullivan's Hollow are fearless, lawless, and illiterate. It is generally believed that Sullivan's Hollow is a small, scattered country village of about five hundred notorious outlaws, a group of people who care nothing for the life of a man, who live with the eternal hope of having the people of other communities bow to them, or who shoot their fellowman down for the fun of seeing him fall.

Dr. Peter Farley defended the people of Sullivan's Hollow in an article for the *Clarion-Ledger*, January 19, 1905, by saying that the Sullivans were, among other things, a kind-hearted, noble, and generous people. His statements prompted this editorial in the *Smith County Reformer* on February 6 of that year:

> We do not attempt to deny that that portion of Smith County has not played its part in the carnival of crime, for so it has. We do, however, condemn most emphatically the tendency of the press and people to lay at the door of the Sullivans the responsibility for almost every act of lawlessness in the County. Generally speaking, the Sullivans are a brave-hearted and generous people. Strangers, passing that way, instead of being roughly treated, as is commonly reported, are the welcome recipients of every hospitality known to the people of that section. We, of course, condemn every form of criminality existing there, and wish that it was otherwise, yet we know that some of Smith County's noblest manhood and womanhood are residents of that persecuted locality, and it is for them, we drop this passing tribute.

Another paper also emphasized this aspect of the Hollow. The Jackson *Clarion-Ledger*, December 15, 1902, printed the following

[9]Howell, "Authentic History," 37.
[10]*Jackson Daily Clarion-Ledger*, November 4, 1903.

editorial entitled "Sullivan's Hollow is a Settlement of Industrious Agriculturists":

> Not many miles from Laurel in Smith County is a tract of country where the piney woods are as yet unassailed by the axe-men and the soft stretches of shaded land are made pleasant by many wandering streams. A country where, by the virtue of strong hands and willing hearts, many fine farms have been won from the wilderness and a set of people dwell who ask nothing more than the reward of their own toil, and need no more than the ground their till produces.

> We refer to Sullivan's Hollow. From the fiery imagination of anxious space writers and newspaper correspondents have come story after story of murder and rapine. In some way—and the custom has become confirmed habit—people speak of Sullivan's Hollow as a place where men walk with arms [weapons] in their hands and murder in their hearts, and where the innocent traveler and wayfarer is in danger of assault and robbery.

> The *Ledger* believes that such statements are cruel, unjust, uncalled for, and unmitigated lies.

> "Give a dog a bad name and hang him." Nearly every male resident of the region under discussion is related to the Sullivans and bears that name. If anything ever does happen, of course it is a Sullivan that is implicated.

> As far as we know, there has never been a case of highway robbery or assault on a traveler or stranger charged to Sullivan's Hollow.

> There has never been a shooting that was not directly due to an attack on womanhood, the outgrowth of some homewreckers action, or [a shooting] by accident in Sullivan's Hollow. There has never been an iota advanced to show that the people of that section of Smith County were not what we believe them to be—as industrious, hospitable as any people in the state.

> Sullivan's Hollow never produced a Matthews or Whit Owens. [Whit Owens from Columbia, Mississippi, was convicted of murder and sentenced to hang in 1902.]

> In the name of common sense and justice, the *Ledger* denounces the defamers of men who have no way to answer back.

> The foul name given this section has even affected the business of the Gulf and Ship Island Railroad, strangers being actually afraid to travel on this line through the section on account of stories that they have heard. This is nonsense.

> We can submit the personal statements of physicians, railroad men, business and professional men of this city in proof that we are right in the statement that Sullivan's Hollow is settled by a class of people who mean harm to no one, who are grossly and unjustly abused, and among whom are many worthy and pleasant families.

R. W. Draugham, the conductor of the Gulf and Ship Railroad, to whom the above facts were submitted before publication, emphatically confirms the *Ledger*'s opinion in this matter and says that he can substantiate the fact that the Sullivans of Sullivan's Hollow have had for years profitable and industrious farms with almost no exceptions. Most of the disorder in this region has been caused by bad men who come in from other points.

These articles, although belligerent and defensive in tone, at least give today's readers the impression that not everyone believed all the yellow journalism.

Some people are quick to believe any description of the type of life in the Hollow. Knowing the Sullivan temperament, there is some truth to the stories about violence; knowing the Sullivan sense of humor, they helped to promote the wild tales. A Sullivan today, with a poker-face, will sell this bill of goods to some fresh-shaven outsider, but if the latter exhibits any doubt, or joins in the fun, the Sullivan will readily admit he was attempting to josh or kid him along; and the Sullivans do love to do just that!

Julius, oldest son of Wild Bill (circa 1930)

PART TWO
Wild Bill Sullivan
1851–1932

Shep Sullivan, grandson of Wild Bill, displaying his grandfather's shotgun.

The Man

AFTER A PERSON has passed from the scene, it is difficult to assess what he was like before he became famous. Details are hidden by the mists of time and the turbulence of the past. So it is with Wild Bill Sullivan. His personality was indeed complex. He was viewed by some as a genteel man; nevertheless, he came to personify in Mississippi all those characteristics of lawlessness and violence. His bawdy sense of humor, his endless fund of stories and tall tales, his love of pranks and foolishness, and, later, his many fights and other acts of violence made him a legend first in Sullivan's Hollow and then throughout Mississippi.

William Cicero Sullivan was the son of Henderson (Hense) and Leah Howell Sullivan. Little is known about his parents; even their birthdates are uncertain. Leah was the first of many Howells to marry a Sullivan. (These two well-known families of Smith County were to become so interwoven that, by the fifth generation in the Hollow, five members of one Howell family married Sullivans.) Hense and Leah lived a short distance above Bunker Hill, near both the Howells and the Sullivans. Bill was the second son and the fourth child of Hense and Leah's ten children.

It is told that Bill was always very close to his older brother Cornelius, commonly called Neece. Born in 1845, Neece was a magnificent specimen, tall and straight and hard-bitten. He was a giant of a man, rugged and ruddy-faced, but with strong, handsome features. He had piercing black eyes and a flowing black beard that reached almost to his waist. He wore his shirt front open the year round.

Neece and Wild Bill were companions in many of the escapades of their later lives. Although Neece was six years older than Bill, it was Bill who became "king of the Hollow." Neece worshiped his brother and was ready to take Bill's side at any time and at any place. There was a special closeness between Bill and Neece that none of the other brothers had.

Bill, a grandson of Thomas Sullivan, was born April 27, 1851. Bill probably did not remember his grandfather, who died in June, 1855, when the lad was only four years old. However, he inherited his grandfather's name and reputation and gave to this area of Mississippi some of the funniest and some of the most violent tales ever to be spun.

Bill probably grew up no differently from most boys of that time in Smith County. He had little or no formal education. In fact, as late as 1905, court records show only his mark (x) rather than a signature. In the 1850s, children in rural areas of Mississippi attended school with little regularity. Boys helped their fathers farm, and girls worked in the homes or in the fields alongside the men. Bill seems to have matured quickly and learned very early to handle his own problems; furthermore, he learned to like the taste of whiskey and soon began to perceive that it was an agent of destruction.

Not much is known about Bill's childhood days. Howell says that Bill helped his father to cultivate the fields, hunt, and fish. "Like most boys, Bill was not so favorably impressed with work, but he could never be regarded as lazy. As a lad, when Bill was sent to plow in the field, he rode the mule to save himself the work of walking to the field. To break him from this habit, one day his brothers placed themselves in a barn loft and when Bill bridled his mule in the stable, mounted and started out of the barn, the brothers dropped a dry cow hide down on him and the mule, causing the mule to break away, jump the corral fence and dismount Bill very suddenly. Bill was not able to plow that day, and the mule never again permitted a rider on him."[1]

When Bill did not want to plow, he would drive his mule to the shade of a tree for a nap. He napped in this way frequently until his father caught onto it. The older Sullivan then tied a small bell on the

---

[1]Howell, "Authentic History," 4.

mule's neck, so that he could listen for it at each step of the mule. Thus Bill was in an inescapable predicament. He plowed many rounds, trying to think how to escape it. At last he retired to the same shade tree around which grass grew, and untied one of his plowlines. To one end of the plowline, he tied the bell, and to the other he tied the mule's tail. The mule began to graze, and to switch his tail from side-to-side, and, simultaneously, the bell began to ring. Bill lay down in the shade and took his usual nap. Such capricious behavior was to characterize him throughout his life.

At eighteen, Bill married Juriah Keyes, daughter of Joe Berry Keyes, who lived first in Covington County and later moved north of Mize. The census of 1870 records the fact that Bill had 156 acres in the Hollow near his father-in-law's land. Bill's fields were productive and easily cultivated, so profits were soon forthcoming from the little farm. By this time of life, men would ordinarily have sown most of their wild oats, but Bill's reckless life had only just begun.

By 1880, the census records show that Juriah considered herself as head of the household. She was twenty-eight with her oldest son Julius being ten; Jane, their daughter, was six; and Jack was two. Very likely, Bill was not at home in 1880, or for reasons that will be explained later, no one wanted the census taker, or any other government official, to know that he was at home. Wild Bill and Juriah had eight children, four boys (Julius, Andrew Jack, Bobbie, and Boyd) and four girls (Mary Jane, Martha Ann, Arizona, and Myrtle).

After they had been married twenty years, their quarters were somewhat crowded, and Bill built a nice six-room house. His farm was always neat and well-kept. Like most of the Sullivans, he had a green thumb. His horses, mules, and cattle were reportedly "out of the ordinary," and his little farm was the envy of all. After his children married and left home, he bought a home in Mize. In his later years, he lived in the homes of some of his children. Julius's second wife, Etta, said that Bill and Juriah lived with them at one time for over three years. Bill died at the home of his son-in-law Thomas Pickering, who married Bill's daughter Martha.

In appearance, Bill was tall and lean; he was probably well over six feet and very graceful. He had the tanned skin of one who leads an outdoor life. He weighed only about 160 pounds. He was described as having a Roman nose, sunken eyes, craggy eyebrows, a wide, firm mouth, a slender neck, and big ears. In his later years, he was gray-haired with a slight cowlick, and he wore a long white mustache. He often wore a large white hat. His grandson Shep Sullivan said Wild Bill's hair had been brown in his younger days, and that his eyes were blue. One newspaper article said he had the white-haired mus-tachioed look of a western marshall. The picture of Wild Bill and his wife, included in this text, was made for an article in the *Commercial Appeal*, June 8, 1930, two years before his death. It reveals him as a slim man with white hair and mustache but with a definite twinkle in his eyes. Photographs published in *Sullivan's Hollow* by Chester Sullivan picture him as a tall man in his early thirties. His hat is tilted back on his head, his legs are crossed, and his eyes are serious.

When family members were asked where he got the name of Wild Bill, two replies were most frequently given. Some said that his title of king of the Hollow and the nickname of Wild Bill were based upon his actions. However, others said he was known during most of his lifetime simply as Bill Sullivan, that "Wild Bill" was added by persons wishing to make a legend of his activities or by writers capitalizing on his notoriety. However, when he dictated his life story to Howell in 1929, he was called by the term "Wild Bill," and, before his death, an article on the Sullivans in the *Commercial Appeal* called him by that name. His present day descendants in the Hollow use that name with an air of pride much like the 1830 American referred to Andrew Jackson as "Old Hickory," or much as a Marine recruit will refer to the toughness of his sergeant. However, in Bill's day, those victims who called him this must have used the term in a different tone.

What kind of man was Wild Bill Sullivan, the legendary king of Sullivan's Hollow? Two characteristics recur in the many reports about him: he was considered a violent man, but he also was a man with a very keen sense of humor.

Bill professed to have never met anyone of whom he was afraid. He was never known to start a fight, but if anyone started any trouble with him, he took care of himself. On the other hand, Neece was habitually getting involved in disputes or starting fights. The usual pattern was that Neece would start the fight, and Bill would finish it. Neece was quiet about what he did, but Bill did not care who knew of his deeds. If challenged, he would fight anyone, anytime, anywhere. If the disagreement could not be settled with fists, then he always had his gun. If such serious trouble developed, Bill knew that he was the fastest man in the Hollow with a gun. People often remarked that Bill and Neece were on the average just as good as anybody else, until they were drinking, and then they were two of the meanest boys in Sullivan's Hollow. According to R. C. Russell, who was their close friend, the two men epitomized all that was good and bad in the Sullivans. Both were scrupulously honest in their business dealing, fiercely loyal to their friends, and courageous to the point of recklessness. Russell said that there was no better people than Bill and Neece, though they would drink whiskey and they would fight![2]

The Sullivans were like other men on the frontier who grew up daily with violence. They were expected to solve problems by their own wits or with their own fists. In many cases the violence was not a deliberate attempt to break or defy the law. It was simply that the violators did not have faith in those designated to enforce the law; or they considered that, in their particular circumstances, the law was not necessary, or perhaps did not apply.

Sullivans never had it easy, nor did they expect an easy way out. They never had much formal schooling, and thus ordinary avenues of recreation, such as reading books, were not open to them. A man's recreation was mostly found in the outdoors—hunting, fishing, or matching his horse, his dogs, and his own strength against that of his neighbors. Even in fun, Sullivans were strongly competitive. Rugged outdoor activities formed the core of their livelihood—farming, logging, and roadwork, all requiring physical strength. Those in Sullivan's Hollow lived by their own peculiar values: pride in one's possessions; a sense of manhood which did not allow a man to be bested; a fierce pride in one's word of honor; and a belief that one could settle his own affairs very well without dependence on anyone else, including the law.

The Sullivan brothers did not consider themselves to be above the law; they just went outside the law to settle difficulties in their own

---

[2]Sullivan, *Sullivan's Hollow*, 38; also see C. Sessions Fant, "Sullivan's Hollow, Smith County" (unpublished manuscript, Mississippi Department of Archives and History, coded 800: Smith County, FEC), 2.

fashion. Thus, Wild Bill was violent because fate led him to violence, because he found from experience that he would survive violent encounters, because he enjoyed it, and because after he gained a reputation for being "mean" it gratified his sense of vanity to maintain that reputation.[3]

Many people say that basically Bill was a gentle person; however, he was quite direct in his relationships with others, almost to the point of rudeness, or so his enemies said. By nature an affable man, Bill was fanatically loyal to his clan and was extremely patriotic to the region in which he lived, remaining anchored firmly to his roots in the Hollow. Even his enemies seldom disliked him as a man. He was neither crooked or venal. He never equated violence with dishonesty. His faults were largely those of temperament. He was overly fond of alcohol, loved adulation, was very independent-minded, and possessed a reckless streak. Like so many frontiersmen, he had a sense of honor which was greatly exaggerated and a controversial means of vengeance. In his attitude towards outsiders or minority groups, he was racist and prejudiced, as were most white Mississippians of his day.

Bill had a remarkable mind, so keen and penetrating that it gave him a broad perspective on a wide range of subjects. He was stimulating to be with, and his forceful personality left an indelible imprint on everyone with whom he associated. He was a big-hearted man, not given to vanity or pompousness, despite his notoriety as a manipulator of man.

His contemporaries described him as a clever, hard-working, enthusiastic man, yet fairly conservative in his thinking. He was gregarious, a marvelous story-teller and lover of tall tales. He also loved to drink, swear, and play poker. All these distinctive qualities made men quake and women swoon. No one can say with complete assurance whether his reputation was acquired or bestowed. Nevertheless, it remains that of a swashbuckling, carefree man whose sense of humor was as keen as his sense of survival. History will always know him simply as "Wild Bill."

---

[3]*Ibid.*, 3.

The Humorist

WILD BILL SULLIVAN is often characterized as a man with a dry sense of humor. The essence of this type of humor cannot be captured with the written word. The nature of the individual himself, the inflection of the words which he said, the vast storehouse of past experiences—all of these must be understood and perceived in their correct relationship in order to see why certain anecdotes about Wild Bill can produce reactions, varying from chuckles to hilarious laughter, even among the Sullivans today. Some episodes, when viewed from the distance of the hundred years that have passed since their occurence, seem to be crude comedy almost bordering on slapstick nonsense. For example, once Bill caught a salesman in the Hollow, proceeded to paint his horse black, and then proclaimed emphatically that the horse belonged to him. This same sense of dry humor exists in Bill's granddaughter, Eula Sullivan Howell, and in his grandson, Shep Sullivan. His love of comical pranks, made even more hilarious after a session with the jug, was passed on to another grandson, Crant Sullivan.

Dovie Sullivan tells the story of how Wild Bill went fishing one day, and upon his return home, his wife Juriah exclaimed: "Why, Bill, are you wet?" Whereupon he replied, deadpan without a trace of a smile, "Well, Juriah, I guess I am. There is no reason for me not to be. I fell into a creek." No scribe, however brilliant, can recount that story and get a laugh. Yet those who know Wild Bill can conjure up the scene vividly. Such is the power of the memory of Wild Bill.

Another tale concerns a stranger who stopped by Bill's house. The visitor said, "I want to stay the night, if I can. Mainly, I want to stay as far away as possible from Wild Bill Sullivan." Without revealing his identity, Bill invited the man in and told Juriah to fix him supper. After supper, he and the stranger sat talking, with Bill treating him with courtesy and respect. The next morning when the stranger started to leave, Bill shook his hand and said, "I'm awfully glad you stayed with me, and if you are ever through this way again, stop and say hello. My name is Wild Bill Sullivan." Bill often told this tale and ended by saying that if he had stuck a knife in the stranger, the man would not have bled one drop.

In his later years, Bill became a member of the Baptist Church, was an excellent citizen, and gave up strong drink. However, he could not escape his own character. In 1930, Howell wrote of him:

> He still goes to Raleigh as he always did during circuit court sessions and today his recitation on the streets of Raleigh of deeds of devilment, and pranks that he has been into, always demand a larger audience than the judge can hope to have. Bill's keen sense of humor accounts for his being the able entertainer he is, with his tales of mischievous pranks never ending. He entertains alike the most illiterate backwoodsman as well as our best educators. He has always known governors, senators, and men of high rank personally, and his visits are always welcomed by them.[1]

Randall Howell, a grandnephew of Bill's, remembers him as a great fisherman but also as a man to be avoided if possible. Bill was a good friend of Randall's father, Judge W. M. Howell. Randall said that although Bill was easily agitated, he was "easy to forget grievances." He told of many times when Bill would come to Judge Howell, wanting the judge to fill out papers so that he could bring a suit against someone who had crossed him. On these occasions Judge Howell would ask Bill to sit on the porch, and they would talk about the prospects of good or bad crops. Then, at the judge's invitation Bill would eat supper and spend the night there. After breakfast the next morning, Judge Howell might say, "Now, Bill, what kind of papers were you wanting me to draw up?" and Bill might stroke his big mustache and say with a droll wit, "Judge, just forget them papers. Just say I came after me something to eat." Then these two grey-

[1]Howell, "Authentic History," 5.

haired fellows would shake hands, each with a twinkle in his eyes, and off Bill would go until the next time he decided to fix up some papers on someone.[2]

Shep Sullivan said his grandfather was one of the gentlest men he ever knew and loved to pull innocent pranks, yet he could laugh at himself. After Shep's mother died in 1914, when he was twelve, Shep lived with his Grandpa Bill and Grandma Juriah for awhile. Shep slept in the same bed with his grandfather, who complained about Shep's tendency to kick during the night. Shep, in an effort to please his grandfather, decided to cure himself of his kicking habit. "I got me a string, tied one end to my big toe and one end to the bed rail, and just waited the next morning until Grandpa started in on his usual complaints about the bad kicking during the night. He didn't do it in a mean way, just picking at me. I was fumbling trying to find that there string when he said, 'Boy, what in the world are you doing?' I showed him my big toe tied to the rail, and he laughed so hard he couldn't get out of bed."[3]

Shep's wife tells of another incident in which Bill's dry wit is exemplified. It seems that when Bill came into the house, he hung his hat and belt on one of the posts that supported the dresser mirror. One day Juriah had put some fresh-cut flowers on the dresser and when Bill went to hang his belt on the post, he knocked over the jar of flowers. He fumed and fussed, saying that a man didn't like flowers and such, and he didn't want to see nary one on his grave when he died.

Another incident recalls the day Bill and Neece went fishing in Cohay swamp around some stumps that stood out in the water. Bill saw a big catfish down in the hollow of a stump and was unable to reach it with his hand. He called Neece over to help him. His plan was for Neece to hold his feet while he went headfirst into the stump and groped for the catfish. Neece would then pull both him and the fish out. However, when Bill had gone all the way down into the stump, Neece let go of his feet and wouldn't pull him out. Bill's arms, head, shoulders, and chest were under water, and he almost drowned before he could let go of the catfish.[4] After then, the very

[2]Interview, Randall Howell, Sullivan's Hollow, Mississippi, 1978.
[3]Interview, Shep Sullivan, Sullivan's Hollow, Mississippi, 1977.
[4]Sullivan, *Sullivan's Hollow*, 40–41.

mention of going catfishing would evoke uncontrollable mirth from the brothers.

In 1963 in the governor's race in Mississippi, legends about the Hollow were used to make a telling political point. Among the candidates was Charles Sullivan, a Clarksdale attorney whose forebears came out of the Hollow. He assured his listeners that a few days in Sullivan's Hollow would do a world of good for Bobby Kennedy and Chief Justice Earl Warren. Old-timers throughout the state laughed at the remark. They knew exactly what Mr. Sullivan implied.[5]

Violence itself was often the basis for the humor. Regular battles were fought at Shiloh Church in Covington County, but the fight best remembered was one in which two men were killed, and Bill's brother Neece was stabbed a dozen times and virtually disemboweled by Tom Chain. Someone pulled Chain off just in time, and Neece, "holdin' his innards with his hands, drug hisself over to his mule and got away." Some twenty years later, Neece's boys came in one night with their clothes in tatters and their bodies bruised and cut from head to foot. They explained, "We been fightin' Tom Chain's boys over to Shiloh Church." Old Neece looked up and said, "Well, if Ah'd known yuh was gonna do that, Ah'd hev told yuh to wear yuh old clothes."[6]

That Wild Bill loved to pull pranks on others, especially such outsiders as traveling salesmen and preachers, seems to be the opinion of almost every person who ever wrote an article on Sullivan's Hollow. It is probable that he not only engaged in the pranks but also, since he was a true Sullivan, he exaggerated the telling of them. Furthermore, the passage of time has transformed stories of the pranks almost into legends.

As early as 1947, *Collier's* published a feature entitled "The Sullivans of Sullivan's Hollow" which pointed out that Wild Bill and his brother Neece loved a good joke; in fact, all the Sullivans did, and even today, the real test in Sullivan's Hollow is whether a person can play a better joke than the other fellow can. The *Collier's* reporter ran into the Sullivan trait of impish delight when he met Fred Sullivan, who, in an interview, squinted, frowned, and said, "Us Sullivans are jest about the meanest people there is. Hain't no crime we

[5]*Jackson Daily News*, July, 1963.
[6]Henderson and Shaw, "Sullivans of Sullivan's Hollow," 82.

ain't committed. We're guilty of 'em all, 'n' we're just so mean we doan' care." When the reporter said he didn't believe it, Fred just sighed with disappointment: "Shucks, ev'y now 'n' then yuh git aholt of a fella who's skitterish, 'n' boy, when we git one like thet, we sure like to lay hit on."

The Sullivans, then and now, are people who enjoy good, clean fun and can get a big laugh out of someone else who gets a good joke on them. They are a set of people who will play a prank on one another just as quickly as they will on anyone else.

Bill and Neece were very much inclined to mischief, and almost daily they pulled pranks on their friends, on strangers, or on one another. Neece lived a short way down the Hollow, and Bill and he would get together often. Each time before executing their plans they would head for Bunker Hill, their "hanging out" place, where they knew their desires could be satisfied. Many fights occurred with resultant loss of lives, and their fights were the beginning of many long, drawn-out family quarrels and feuds.

One of these occurred at a time when Bill and Neece were invited to have dinner with the owner of the sawmill in Bunker Hill. Some of Bill and Neece's enemies were also invited. Not being pleased with the guests present at this dinner, Neece rushed for a knife, and asked Bill to help him clear the house. Bill replied, "Do it yourself and let me eat," at which Neece jerked out Bill's shirttail and cut it off. Bill slashed Neece on the shoulders and arms with his knife. The guests, seeing the floor becoming spotted with Neece's blood, cleared out quickly without further controversy.

Another incident typifies their mischief and violence. One day when the family preacher was to visit their father's home for dinner, Bill and Neece, with their two sisters, were to prepare dinner and entertain him. For some reason the rest of the family were not at home. The boys decided that a good joke would be to prevent the sisters from preparing the dinner. They placed a long ladder beside the house and climbed to the housetop to look over the farm and surrounding country. After a few minutes, they came down hurriedly and told the girls they had just seen a pack of wolves on the farm. The girls, very much alarmed, were allowed to climb up to the housetop and see the wolves. While they were on the roof, Bill and Neece removed the ladder and then hid it. Thus when the preacher came for dinner, he found only the two girls at home, both perched upon the roof of the house, and no dinner prepared.

Another episode occurred when Bill and Neece were young. It was the boys' chore to bring the geese to the well for watering. On one cold day, they decided to surprise their mother by making the geese appear to be very hot. They caught the geese one at a time, opened their mouths and placed a short piece of wood the size of a matchstick between the upper and lower mouth which would hold their mouths open. The geese, therefore, appeared to pant. The boys drove the geese to the well and, when their mother was summoned to draw water for them, she quickly observed that they were very hot and hurried with the water. But to her surprise, the geese would not drink nor cool off. After examining the geese she found the trouble, but Bill and Neece had gone.

Sullivan's Hollow, after its name became famous, was rarely pestered with peddlers, although one happened through once in a while. A Bible salesman once reached the Hollow and paid a visit to the Henderson Sullivan home. Before the salesman had time to introduce his wares, he was suspected to be a peddler, and Bill and Neece raised a panel of rail fence, poked the salesman's head through the crack, and let the fence down on him. There was barely room in the fence crack for his neck. They then placed a beehive near him, leaving the bees to become fearfully familiar with the peddler. After a few minutes, they released the peddler who thought he might find a better sale for Bibles elsewhere.

Bill's father was once having trouble with something stealing his chickens at night. He suspected 'coons and 'possums as the thieves. He was watching his flock very closely one night when Bill and Neece sneaked to the chicken house, quietly took an old hen from the roost, tied a coonskin over her and set her loose. Of course, she made a great outcry and ran about the premises struggling with the coonskin. At last the hen had shaken the skin loose except for a string tied to one of her feet. The skin dragged after her. Meanwhile the boys' father had gotten out of bed and was trying to shoot whatever was after the hen. Of course, he saw the coon after the hen and shot several times at it, but some of his shot killed the hen. Not until he had examined the hen did he know that he had been the butt of this joke.

At another time when Bill and Neece were tired from plowing all day and the girls, who had been hoeing nearby, were also tired, a controversy came up over whether the boys or girls should ride the mules to the barn, a long distance. Their father intervened and permitted the girls to ride. The boys strode away towards home when this decision was rendered, with Bill carrying a trace chain home in his hand. Thinking it wasn't fair to allow the girls to ride home when he had done the plowing, he hid beside the road in a narrow neck of woods. As the girls came close to him he rattled the chain slightly. One of the mules stopped, threw up his head, pointed his ears, and snorted. The other mules became excited also. After a few moments during which Bill kept quiet, the mules decided to pass the noise. When only a few steps were taken by the mules, there was another rattle by Bill. The mules were more excited than ever, and they started to run. The jumping threw the girls to the ground, and the mules ran away. Bill sneaked home another way, and the girls' chances of riding home were ended.

Once while plowing, Bill and Neece found a woodpecker's nest about twenty feet up in a dead field pine. The bird flew about the tree making much noise and commotion. The boys thought the old lady peckerwood was parading before her young, and trying to teach them great contempt and pride. Neece couldn't stand this humiliation; therefore, he planned to climb up and take the young out of the nest and pass some humiliation back to the old proud-looking bird. Accordingly, and with much effort, by hugging the old slick pine he worked himself to the hole where the nest was. Upon reaching it, he was entirely exhausted. Reaching for the young birds, he felt a nestful of cold softness that did not feel much like young birds. He quickly withdrew his hand, and following his hand out of the hole was an ugly-looking chicken snake. Neece descended to the ground about as fast as gravity would pull him. After sliding down the tree a few feet, the friction caused so much heat that he had to release his hug around the tree and take to the air. Accordingly he landed in the plowed ground with great force, but with no injuries except to his pride.

Even though Mississippi was widely known for its racial prejudice, very few of the Sullivan episodes involve blacks. It is generally agreed that very few blacks were welcome in the Hollow. Most of the ones who lived there in the latter nineteenth century were descendants of family slaves. Once Neece and Bill caught a black man, tied a bundle of bobwire to his back, and made him get down on all-fours and crawl a mile, before telling him to leave the Hollow.

Both brothers were shot, stabbed, and wounded on many different occasions. At one time Neece was wounded with birdshot and remarked as he got on his horse and started home that it was an insult to anyone to be shot with such small shot. At another time, a black man filled Bill's breast with birdshot. After this, he walked into the black's house, lit his pipe and started to smoke, but the loss of blood made him sick, and he was carried home by his brothers.

In 1880, Bill and Neece ran afoul of the law in the Bryant Craft murder case, which will be told later. They took to the woods for about four years. Even then, their love of pranks continued to play an important part in their lives. Wild Bill tells it best in his own words.

> Me and Neece shore had lots o' fun when we was lyin' out. I recollect one night when we was a fixin' to camp out and sleep in the woods we had a little fire built and Neece had stretched out by the side uv it and went to sleep. I wanted to pull some kind o' prank on 'im 'cause 'twern't but a few days fo' that he had pushed me off'n a foot log, into the creek. I happened to think about a big chicken snake we had killed that day and was not but about a quarter of a mile back from the fire. I slipped back and got it and when I got back Neece was sleeping like a log. I tied the snake to his foot and got over on the other side of the fire from him and shot my gun twice and hollered "snake." Neece jumped up and when he drawed his foot up to get up the snake follered along arter it. Neece tried his best to jump out 'o the way o' the snake but it looked to him lack it was jumpin arter him. Neece throwed his hat off and started to run out across a little ol' fiel' but soon foun' the snake was tied to him. He eased back to the fire and said, "I'll just be damned if I don't keep you awake all night, just for that."
>
> Another time me and Neece was a' settin' on a log by the road and I told Neece I was goin't have some fun. I said the first one comes down this road is a' goin' to dance for us. I hadn't hardly more'n said it when I seed a' old man a' comin' down the road a' ridin' a horse and when he got close to us I ast him where he was goin' he said, "to Mize." I said, "Did you ever dance any?" "Not much" he said. "Well, we want to see you get down off that horse and try it." He looked at me for a minit and didn't move. I said "You must not know who I am. If you don't know, I'll tell you. I am Wild Bill Sullivan, an' I mean fur you to git down and shake your feet." He didn't hesitate this time. He danced 'till the sweat was a' pouring off his face, and then I said, "That will do." The old man said, "Before you told me who you was, I had a' min' not to dance, but now, if you won't tell

anybody about this prank in Mize, I'll give you a good drink o' whiskey." I said, "I shore won't tell it." I put my gun down and he reached in his saddle pocket to get what I thought was the whiskey. The first thing I seed a' comin' out was the handle of a big navy pistol. He said, "Did you ever dance any?" I said, "No, but by golly I am goin' at it right now." (Here there was a loud laugh by all) "When I had danced 'till my knees began to wobble, he said, "That will do." We shook han's an' he went on down the road and me and Neece went back to the woods.

Neece had the laugh on me arter this so finally one day he sez, "I'll show you how to pull a trick and get away with it." I said "Well, let me see it." We walked on down through the woods 'till we came to a fiel' where an old man was a' plowin' a gray mule. Neece walked up an ast him where he got his mule. He said he bought him more'n five years ago. "Well don't you know that all Sullivans turn to gray mules and never die?" He said, "Wa'al I've heard that." Neece then walked up to the mule's head, caught hol o' his ears and whacked 'em off with his knife and said, "I just wanted to mark this old mule so we would allus know him as a Sullivan." The old man's eyes run out an' he jerked his hat off and throwed it down on the groun' an' begin to cuss. Neece pulled out his gun an' walked up to 'im and said, "You must be hot." Neece grabbed hold o' his overalls and told the ol' man to pull 'em off so he could cool off. By us a' helpin' 'im a little he was soon pantless. Neece throwed his overalls up in a tree and made him go to plowin', with his gun. As he went on down the row a' plowin' in his shirttail, me and Neece turned 'roun and went on 'bout our business.

Later Bill and Neece gave up hiding, but their fun continued. Bill recalled a party the Hollow folk threw for them not long after their return from the woods:

They was goin' to have a contest between me and Neece and two brothers o' ourn, Jack and Henry. The one that told the biggest lie was to have a quart of whiskey as a prize. Jack had the first chance and he opened up and said, "Well, I don't drink whiskey." I knowed this would be hard to beat for he liked whiskey better'n I did. Henry said, "Well, you all know me better'n to tell a lie for a quart o' whiskey." Everybody busted out in a big laugh when he said that. Neece told 'em, "I don't like nor drink whiskey, so I am not goin' to start up this late in life." I was so tickled that I couldn't even think of a lie.

I studied a minit then told 'em, "Well all of them have told you the truth." They reached out and handed me the quart o' whiskey.[7]

Once, after Wild Bill had come out of hiding, he was in the hotel cafe in Raleigh. The proprietor asked him to pay an old debt that dated from several years before. Bill asked what he owed money for,

[7]Howell, "Authentic History," 20–24.

and the proprietor said that he owed for his bed and board. Bill paid the amount that the man asked, but then went upstairs and came down with a mattress across his shoulder. When the owner protested, Bill commented, "Well, you said that I owed for board and bed. I've already had my board, so now I'm getting my bed." Bill took the mattress home and kept it.

Only a few of Bill's pranks involved his brother Henderson, or "Henry," who was six years younger than Bill. However, one story tells that after Henry married Mary Eubanks, Bill went to spend the night at their house. Bathrooms were unheard of in that day, and the home of the newlyweds was fairly unfamiliar to Bill. When he had to get up during the night to go out behind the shed, he tied a string to the foot of his bed to find his way back safely. Henry caught on to what Bill had done, so he untied the string and tied it to the foot of the bed where his wife lay. Then as Bill crawled into that bed, Henry began to rant at Bill for trying to sneak into his wife's bed. Of course, they both got as much fun out of retelling the story later as they did when it first occurred.

Before the advent of modern machinery, counties used to hire individuals and their mules to work on the roads. In his later years, Bill sometimes hired out himself and his mule Ap. Henry had a store at Mize, and Bill would leave his lunchbox, a small lard bucket, there. Bill would plan his work so that he would be back at his brother's store in time for his noonday meal of meat and biscuit, cold baked sweet potatoes, or whatever his wife Juriah had packed.

One morning after Bill left to go work on the roads, Henry took the lunch out of Bill's pail, and substituted in its place a dirty dishtowel and wet dishrag. Some versions maintain that the pail contained fresh cow manure. When Bill came in to eat his lunch, and found the rags there, he fumed and cussed because of Juriah's mix-up. Henry did not tell what he had done, but shortly thereafter Bill learned who had pulled the prank on him. He never revealed to Henry that he had learned the truth, but he quietly began to plot his revenge.

Bill's opportunity soon came. He had a son named Boyd who was about to leave Mize to return to his home in Chicago. Bill got Boyd to write a letter to Henry and to mail it from Jackson, the capital of Mississippi. The letter stated that the government had found out that Henry was selling more sugar than he was allowed under the rationing system effective in World War I. Furthermore, the letter said that a state inspector would be down on the train on a given day and would go over Henry's books with him. The letter considerably upset Henry, perhaps because he actually was guilty of the infraction of the rules. On the day that the inspector was scheduled to arrive, Henry put on his best clothes and went down to the depot to meet him. Bill strolled along casually and slipped up near to where Henry was standing. Just before the train pulled in, Bill said to Henry, "I guess now when Juriah fixes me something to eat in my bucket, it'll be there when I go to eat if."[8]

The truth about Wild Bill has become so entwined with legend that it is difficult to separate the two. In writing of Sullivan's Hollow, John K. Bettersworth of Mississippi State University did not try to do so. He referred to the way Mississippians speak "with genuine delight of the numerous feuding Sullivans of Sullivan's Hollow, whose capital was Mize, where the best watermelons and some of the liveliest tall tales in Mississippi were produced."[9]

Dovie and her husband Shep Sullivan. They are descendants of Thomas Sullivan, and Dovie Sullivan is the present occupant of the log house in the Hollow.

[8]Interview, Dovie Sullivan, Sullivan's Hollow, Mississippi, 1978.
[9]Bettersworth, *Mississippi*, 509.

The King
of the Hollow

ALTHOUGH BILL did have a sense of humor that led him to play jokes upon other people, this same reckless behavior easily turned into violence of a more harmful and illegal nature. Before he was twenty-one years old, he was wanted by the sheriff for murder. Furthermore, he was responsible for his Uncle Loden fleeing the Hollow. He was feared by most people, condemned by some, and admired by others.

To most Mississippians, Bill typified life in Sullivan's Hollow. He drank heavily, cursed when drunk, fought anyone who disagreed with him, ruled his clan with knife and gun, and killed several men. Undoubtedly, he was the most picturesque of the Sullivans, and certainly the most violent and notorious of the clan. Many believed that it was he who gave the Hollow a bad name and the one who committed the most of the meanness. These views prevailed during his lifetime. As time passed and the stories became exaggerated, he became the subject of many newspaper stories. Yet he seems to have been a veritable enigma even to those who knew him best. Interviews with his son, daughter-in-law, grandsons, and neighbors proved contradictory and inconclusive.

Boyd Sullivan, Bill's youngest son (1894–1979), said his father was the finest man around. "Pa looked after me. He never whipped me," Boyd said. "I didn't know what a drink of whiskey looked like until I was twenty-one." Boyd noted that, although Wild Bill had a reputation for being mean and bad, he saw his father fight only with his fists. He told of the time when Wild Bill had invited a peddler out to their house. "Well, my father had been drinking when he got out there. One of the traces had come loose on this old peddler's wagon, and when he got to our house, he told me to fasten the trace. I did it; I really didn't mind doing it for the fella. My father got real mad at the peddler for ordering me to do it; so he pulled this peddler out of the wagon, slapped him on the jaw, and told him to drive on."[1]

Judge Mac Kimbrough of Itta Bena also shared this paradoxical view of Wild Bill. Although the judge acknowledged that Bill was an outlaw, he said that Bill was one of those lusty pioneers who pushed back our frontiers, a man who would go through hell to help a friend or get an enemy. The unusual friendship between the dignified Judge Kimbrough and the uninhibited head of the Sullivans traced back to a period when vandals repeatedly burned out the trestles of the Gulf and Ship Island Railroad through Sullivan's Hollow. Although it was assumed that the culprits were Sullivans, there seemed no way to catch them or prove the accusation. To put an end to the vandalism, Judge Kimbrough did a strange thing. He visited Wild Bill, went hunting with him, casually turned over $500 to him, and asked for Wild Bill's word that no more trestles would be burned out. No more trestles burned. The judge and Wild Bill became life-long friends.

In fact, in 1900, when the judge's son Will took a walking tour of Mississippi, the judge told him to look up his old friend. When young Will Kimbrough arrived in Sullivan's Hollow, he was warmly welcomed by Wild Bill and his family and enjoyed their friendliness so much that he stayed four days, fishing and hunting with the Sullivan boys.[2]

Shep Sullivan said his grandfather was always honest, a very fair man. Shep's wife Dovie said that he was "right jolly," good company, and very entertaining. She remembered that he liked to rock the babies on his knee and that he would always make it a point to speak to the children. She added that "he knowed everybody. He was nothing like everyone said he was, or that he had the name of being. Maybe he killed some people—I guess he did; they said he did; he never talked about it when I knew him."[3]

[1]Lonnie Wheeler, "Sullivan's Hollow—Fighting Family Heritage," *Jackson Clarion-Ledger*, October 31, 1977, p. 16A.
[2]Ray M. Thompson, "Horseback in Mississippi," *Gulfport-Biloxi Daily Herald*, November 9, 1960.
[3]Interview, Dovie Sullivan, 1977.

Bill's daughter-in-law Etta Wallace Sullivan recalls him as being a fair man who never interfered with other people's affairs, but that when he did speak, he was listened to.

Others in the valley definitely viewed him as an outlaw, one greatly to be feared. One of the few men who had a run-in with Wild Bill and still lived to tell the tale was lanky, grey-haired W. D. Stubbs, who lived just south of the Hollow in Covington County. Stubbs was courting a girl in Sullivan's Hollow. To impress her, he was carrying a bouquet of wild flowers. As his horse rounded a bend, Stubbs came upon a wagon, and "settin' there in the wagon with a jug o' whiskey was Wild Bill, 'n' him jest as full as the jug." Wild Bill demanded that Stubbs have a drink, but Stubbs claimed he was late already and could not take time. "All of a sudden," Stubb relates, "he lay over 'n' come up with his pistol leveled at me, sayin', 'Hev a drink with me, or Ah'll start shootin', and Ah'll start shootin' that bunch o' flowers outa yuh han'!'" Stubbs thrust the bouquet from him, reared up his horse and got away. "Wild Bill sent word next day that he was sorry about hit. He said if Ah'd jest come to Mize he'd get down on his knees 'n' beg my forgiveness in the street. Ah thought maybe he would, 'cause he really was a fine fellow, but on second thought, Ah decided not to risk hit."[4]

Wild Bill's first serious fight occurred when he was sixteen years old. Bill had finished the meager schooling available in his time and place. One day he was riding past the home of Pad Speed (probably Patrick D. Speed of Covington County). Speed did not exactly like the pose assumed by Bill. Speed came out and ordered Wild Bill off his horse and said that he was going to whip hell out of him. Being young, Bill was seemingly an easy mark for Speed, yet hardships had matured him, and he was lithe as a deer. Bill immediately dismounted and engaged Speed in a fist fight which left Speed limping, his clothes torn, and his nose and face bleeding. Of course Speed could not endure this kind of humiliation from a youngster and he was determined that his whipping should not end the dispute.

A few days passed before Speed met Bill again while attending church at an all day meeting in the Hollow. Speed asked Bill to accompany him down the road away from the church so that their trouble could be thrashed out. Bill, without any indication that he

[4]Henderson and Shaw, "Sullivans of Sullivan's Hollow," 83.

was worried, accepted the challenge and followed Speed. Several people nearby sensed that there was to be a scrap and followed the two men. Out of sight of the church, Speed threw off his coat. Bill cast aside his knife and gun, held out his fists and remarked, "These two malls is all I need to satisfy you." Speed sprang onto Bill and had him down before he knew the fight had started. By this time Bill was getting into a bad humor. He raised to his all-fours, sprang upright, and caught Speed on the face with a terrific right, almost bending him back to the ground. After another second's hesitation to balance himself, Bill attacked him. The struggle ended in almost the same way as their first fight. After a few minutes of rolling and mauling, Speed said "Enough." Then and there Speed "handed the belt" to Wild Bill.[5]

After this successful whipping of Pad Speed, Bill's head was so "swelled up" he thought two guns and a knife would be stylish for him. They were accordingly secured and worn.

Bill's next encounter was with Gabe Chain, son of William and Melinda Chain. It occurred on a Sunday at Shiloh Church, which is near Sullivan's Hollow but in Covington County. Frank Gibbeons, son of Louisa Gibbeons and brother of Emily, who was married to Neece, went to church with Bill that day. After arriving at the church they became separated. Gabe Chain began to follow Gibbeons, trying to pick a fight with him. Gibbeons would not fight unless he was forced. Then he was hard to stop. When Bill met Gibbeons, he told Bill that Gabe Chain wanted to start a row. Bill said, "Well Gib, can't you help him get it started?"

Later, they saw Chain standing under a shade tree, talking to some of his gang. Approaching them, Bill said, "Chain, I hear you are looking for a fight and by ginger, I want to know if you are." They fought, and soon Chain was so fatigued that he began to back away. Chain had bitten a wound on Bill's arm which spurted blood in his eyes, and Sullivan dived for Gabe again. This time there was even more blood. Bill beat Gabe until he was exhausted, knocked him down, spat on him and said, "Now bite that." The fight was over, but Chain's desire for revenge grew, and this feeling finally brought on the bloodiest fight the Hollow ever knew.[6]

[5]Howell, "Authentic History," 8.
[6]*Ibid.*, 9.

This fight is known in Smith County as the battle of Shiloh. Differing versions of the fight exists. However, in 1929, Wild Bill told it to Howell, who recorded it thusly:

One beautiful Sunday morning in May, when the Shiloh church bell pealed out notice to dwellers of Sullivan's Hollow that it was time for the monthly meeting to begin, which was an invitation to some people for religious worship, to some folk for a big feast from the long dinner table, but to others who held the big fighting records, it was an invitation to begin to execute their plans. Gabe Chain and his gang, composed of Chains, Dykes, and Rutlings, had been meeting the previous week at the old Bunker Hill mill to plan for the day. They decided this particular Sunday to put Neece Sullivan beneath the sod. Neece wore a long mustache and for this reason was called the "Mare's Tail." They planned that before the sun went down to "pull the Mare's Tail." Some sources say that Neece's wife was being enticed by Gabe, and that Neece had found out about it.

Gabe and his gang rode their horses along towards the Shiloh Church not anticipating the loss of any of their gang in the execution of the plans to do away with Neece. However, in the event that any member of the gang did die, the other members were to sing and dance at his funeral. Wild Bill, Neece, Dan Hathorn, son of E. N. and Elizabeth Hathorn, and Frank Gibbeons had reached the church before the other gang arrived, and soon were informed that the Chains would be on hand that day to deal with them. The Sullivan gang, not being afraid of the devil himself, was not alarmed. Furthermore, fighting was the excitement that they craved. Dinner time came and both gangs were present. The gangs began to move about, restlessly, seeking advantages and information as to the other's movement.

Some of both gangs had to go to a nearby spring for water after dinner. Both parties had carried their liquor too, and proceeded to uncork and drink their whiskey. Neece and Dan Hathorn had ridden their horses to a point a little downstream from the spring, and upon their return from the bushes which grew around the watering place for horses, most of the Chain gang came onto them with knives and guns. A rush was made for Neece, to pull "the Mare's Tail," but Neece managed to keep them whipped off with a riding whip. By this time Dan Hathorn had ridden through them, dismounted, and returned to assist Neece. The balance of the Sullivan gang, being on the lookout for trouble, reached Neece about the time Hathorn did. Chain had Neece pulled off his horse, and his men were beating and cutting him. The Sullivans began using their knives and clubs, and, soon, some of the Chains' followers were temporarily out. The men were so close together in their fighting that it was difficult to tell who was who. Their faces and clothes were bespattered with blood, and bruises disfigured them to some extent. Gabe Chain was now cut so badly that the loss of blood forced him to begin to faint.

As he fell, he said "don't forget our task," meaning "pull the Mare's Tail." The continuous loss of blood left Gabe cold and stiff. Being their leader, the loss of Gabe was serious to the Chain gang, but they continued to fight, though severely weakened. Pete Dykes, another of the Chain gang, was the next to fall. The loss of blood caused him to weaken and stagger, and he fell backward to the roadside, dropped his knife, and reached for support from a tree. However, he was too weak, so he slumped to the ground. When one of the Chain gang asked Pete if he was hurt much, Dan Hathorn of the Sullian gang said, "You damn right he is hurt. He is dead as hell."

Neece, by this time, had been cut and bruised so much that the loss of blood caused him to retire from the fight. Dan Hathorn thought Neece was dead, but when he picked him up to move him back out of the way, he found him still alive. The Chain gang wanted their object of the fight—Neece—and an attempt was made to take him away from Hathorn. Hathorn kept them back by pulling two guns and saying, "If you touch him, you are dead men." This remark, plus the death of Dykes and their leader, Gabe Chain, caused them to quit the fight.

Neece was taken back to the spring, and his wounds washed. Wounds across his abdomen were such as to permit his men to pull his entrails through and wash them, which they did. More than an hour later, in preparation to carry Neece to a doctor for treatment, they bound Neece up around the stomach. Neece rode his horse to the doctor. [Author's note: Ms. Myra Rice of Texas says her grandmother sewed up Neece's wound.] After the doctor had sewn him up, Neece climbed onto a nearby stump, and proceeded to imitate a rooster by putting his fingers into his armpits, and crowing loudly. The Chain gang did not "pull the Mare's Tail" but, in their attempt to do so, they had lost two of their gang, Chain and Dykes, and the others were severely cut and beaten. The Sullivan gang did not lose any of their number, but received many deep gashes from knives.

The following afternoon the same church bell pealed out unmistakably sad tones. After ceremonies were over and the two men burried, the rest of the Chain gang danced and sang over their graves as they had promised to do.[7]

Although the battle at Shiloh added to Bill's reputation as a fighter, the fight that made Wild Bill a notorious character in the Hollow was the one that occurred with Bryant Craft. Bill told Howell that it took place in this fashion:

One cold Friday morning, while all of the regular gang was a' hangin' 'round by Uncle Loden's house at Bunker Hill, he asked us to an all day log rollin' the next day and he was gwine give a big frolic arter the work was through. This sounded mighty good to us and we was anxious for Satidy

[7]*Ibid.*, 15–18.

to come on. Some uv us didn't have enough whiskey to last through the frolic, so we got out that e'nin and made things ready for the nex day. Soon Satidy mornin' the crowd started gatherin' at Uncle Loden's house and account the weather bein' chilly he give us all a big drank o' whiskey. This made us all feel good and prosperous and we was then all ready for a big day's work. The mornin' past fo' we knowed it and soon 'at enin' we had logs rolled. All we has to do then was be patient and wait for the dance to come off, so we kept on tankin' up on our whiskey and by the time the old fiddlers came in we was all good and ready. Finally the dance got started and we got to slingin' our partners. Once in awhile we would git out to take another drank. The shindig went on about three or four hours when me and Bryant Craft picked out the same gal to dance with. [Some say the cause of enmity was that Bill was having an affair with Bryant's sister.] I thought bein' I was so big a fighter and important in the country that I ought to have the gal but Craft didn't see it just lack I did so we went outside to settle the trouble. There we was staggering around nearly drunk and o' tryin' to fight. Neece was out there so I handed him my gun and when I started on Craft I noticed he had a knife in his han'. I struck him then with a piece of plank I found a' lyin' close by but I dropped it out o' my han' and as I reached for it agin Craft stabbed me several times in the back. They all got us apart from one another and we was took to a doctor for treatin' and while we was there we made up and buried the hatchet.

It wasn't lon arter that till we had another run in. Me and Neece had been to Mize one day and as we was a goin' back to Bunker Hill we passed Bryant Craft and his brother by the side o' the road. They yelled at us but we didn't ack like we seed 'em. We went on down the hill but we noticed that the Crafts was coming on down the road too, a' follerin' us. They begin to shoot off their guns but we didn't pay 'em any min' and when we got to the mill I see Bryant Craft a' easin' 'roun a rail fence to where I was. I knowed it wouldn' do for us to wait and see what was goin' to be done so I raised my double barrel and shot him through the crack o' the fence. He died, but the other Craft got away.

The sheriff was sent word o' this shooting but me and Neece had made up our minds we would not never go to jail, so we took to the woods, and stayed there for more'n two years. The sheriff come down to Bunker Hill but he didn' make any search for us because he knowed it wern't any use. We was told he 'lowed to catch us if we didn' stay hid mighty close. We wern't very careful though because lots of people knowed where we was, and when we knowed the sheriff was not aroun' to look fur us we would stay all night with somebody and eat a meal or two. Sometime we would stay down on the Hollow and sometimes up above Mize where my wife's folks lived and sometimes we would stay any place we wanted to most, but of course we was on the lookout all the time. Heap o' times while we was in the woods we would see a manhunt, none of 'em ever tried to arrest us. Ever' time we went to somebody's house to stay all night we took 'em a turkey or two. I don't guess a day ever passed what we didn't kill a turkey. Me and Neece started one time to keep a' count o' all the turkeys we killed but when we got up to more'n eighty we quit countin' 'em. I don' know how many deer me and Neece killed. More'n a thousan' I guess. I recollect lots o' days we killed three deer and seven turkeys. We didn't have anything to do but hunt so the game had to be mighty sharp to git by us.

The sheriff, John Mize, would make a little search for us about once a' month but I don' think he wanted to ketch us though because lots o' times the searchers seed us and would go on and pay no 'tention to us. The sheriff finally put out a reward fur us and also said if he knowed of anybody givin' us somethin' to eat and ammunition he would put a heavy fine on 'em. This didn't keep me and Neece from gettin' what we wanted though. One night we stayed at a Mr. Spell's house and while we was eatin' breakfast a Mr. Gentry walked in. Spell knowed this man always told ever' thing he could fin' out but I told Mr. Spell to not let it worry him for I would take care o' that matter. We stayed aroun' the house fur a good while and when Gentry started to leave I picked up my gun an' follered him down the road a piece. As quick as we got away from the house, I took Gentry by the arm an' said, "Hol' on a minit, you have got the name o' tellin' ever' thing you know but if you tell anybody you saw me and Neece at Spell's it will be the last time you ever told anything." Believe me he shore did take me at my word, too. (A chuckle at the joke).

One day after we had been a' hidin' out for more'n a year and a half my wife's father told me and Neece that Sheriff John Mize wanted to see us. I told him to tell the Sheriff where we would be and if he wanted to see us it would be alright for him to come where we was. I also told him to tell the Sheriff that he had better not be tryin' to trick us into gettin' caught for that might not work. In a day or two I saw the Sheriff comin' through the woods and me and Neece went to where he was. We soon learnt he wanted us to go and give ourselves up to the law. We told the Sheriff that we was not goin' to give up. He said we would be turned loose without ever bein' give any trouble. We told the Sheriff that we was not afraid of trouble and also told him he had better keep his searchin' party out of the woods a' lookin' for us. I told him that my old gun barrel was used so much that it was wore out so thin it was get'n bent lots o' times but it will still shoot jist as good as ever, and I wasn't afraid to use it nuther. The Sheriff kept on talkin' and finally said, "Well Bill, I'll tell you what to do. You and Neece stay on the north side o' the road for two weeks and I'll search for you on the south side; then the next two weeks you can go on the south side and I'll hunt for ;you on the north side." He told me not to tell this to a soul and he wouldn't nuther.

It wasn't long before the Sheriff sent us word that he wanted to see us again. I told them to tell him to come back to the same place he met us before and shore 'nuff the next day he came. He told us lots of people had found out he had talked to me and Neece and he would have to make some honest attempt to get us from then on. I told him that didn't make much difference to us as we could take care of ourselves. The Sheriff tried to get us to go on and give up. He said we ought to be willin' to give up after we had been out more'n two years time. I told him we wern't ready to give up and never would be. He said, "Well, I can't fool with you all any longer. You will have to look out for yourselves." I guess he thought this was goin' to bluff us, but we might' quick got him told we were not going to be caught by him nor any of his gang. I told him he better remember we was goin' to do just as you told us—'look out for ourselves.' I told him that I also thought we could well do that for we had done it so far and never failed yet. The Sheriff then got up and started off and said, "Well Bill, I guess you and Neece better go turkey huntin' out in the swamp next Saturday, and if anything else happens I'll send you word." The Sheriff made three or four more searches, but he always sent us word beforehand.

Bryant Craft's brother finally sent me and Neece word to come on out'n the woods. He said all the bitter feelin's had been forgot and they were ready to be friends. Knowin' Craft just like I did, I knowed he meant every word of it, so me and Neece come out and made friends with Crafts and then we went and done as we pleased.[8]

Others in the Hollow said that once during their time as fugitives the brothers went to Texas to get some rest. The legend reports that in a store there, Bill picked up a newspaper and saw his own picture staring up from the front page. He showed it to Neece. They exchanged glances but no words and left Texas immediately, returning to where they felt safest, Cohay Swamp.

Loden Sullivan, a brother of Bill's father, disputed Bill's right to rule the Hollow. Wild Bill and Neece had considerable trouble convincing their Uncle Loden that they should be permitted to do as they pleased in Sullivan's Hollow. They liked to brag about their many exploits. They often told their listeners that their uncle was the man whom they had made dance for them while they were hiding out; also, he was the man who plowed for them in his shirttail. Loden did not seem to understand that these things were only jokes and said, "Some day you are going to meet your match. You are going to make one step too many. If you start any of your foolishness around me, you will might' quickly find out who that man is too."

"Well, we have never been stopped and don't ever expect to be," Bill retorted. Bill then yanked out his gun, threw two bottles high in the air and burst them both before they hit the ground. "Now, who

[8]*Ibid.*, 25–28.

in hell are we afraid of?" he said. Bill replaced his gun, and he and Neece caught their horses and leisurely rode off. Late in the afternoon of the same day as they were riding back toward Bunker Hill, they noticed their Uncle Loden plowing in a field nearby. Bill said, "Well, Neece, I guess we better get over the fence and go see what we can do with Loden." "Yes, I think we ought to go get him to tell us who that brave fellow is he was telling us about this morning," said Neece. They dismounted, tied their horses to the fence, and walked out across the field to Loden. They noticed he had a gun stuck in his belt, but as they were looking for trouble, they expected some such preparation by Loden; in fact, they were glad to see that he was armed. Bill made Loden raging mad when he said, "Well Loden, we have come over just to let you know who we are. But before we do, I'll say to you just as we say to all, we take no chances!" Loden started up his mule and went on plowing. Bill and Neece followed for some distance, kicking Loden with each step. Soon they stopped the mule, and pointed a gun at Loden. Then they mounted him on one mule, they got on the other, and rode down to the Bunker Hill pond where they "soused" Loden in it. When Loden stuck up his head for air, they asked, "Now, who is that bad man you were telling us about?" Loden hated to give in, but he knew that if his wife and children were ever to know what became of him, or where he went, he must give in.

Early on the next day while passing Loden's house, Bill and Neece decided to visit with him. Loden ordered them not to enter his yard, but Bill walked on in. Loden went into a room for his shotgun. As Bill was going into the house, Loden was coming out at the door, and Loden struck his head with the shotgun. Bill temporarily was staggered by the blow. When Loden saw Neece entering the yard, Loden threatened to shoot him. Of course Neece did not have "stop" in his vocabulary. He continued his advance toward the house, so Loden fired a load of small shot into his chest. Neece opened his shirt to examine the wound. "I've a good mind to kill you for shooting me with small shot!" he cried to Loden. Neece went into the house, got Bill, and they rode on down to Bunker Hill.[9]

A short time after this incident, a rumor was spread that Bill and Neece had cut Loden to pieces with knives. Loden was in very criti-

---

[9] *Ibid.*, 10

cal condition. As the people gathered into the home to offer their assistance to him, they talked about Bill and Neece's taking such cowardly advantage of Loden to steal in on him at night and get revenge. Bill and Neece shortly came by to see Loden and informed everyone that they had nothing to do with cutting their uncle, and that Loden knew that they had never been afraid to face trouble openly; it was not characteristic of them to do such a thing. When Loden became strong enough to speak, his first words were, "Whether I live or die, I want everybody to know that the cutting was not done by Bill and Neece, for they had nothing to do with it. It was someone else's dirty work."[10]

Loden did not die of these wounds, however. He moved out of the Hollow, died in 1898, and was buried in a cemetery near Bassfield, Mississippi. After Loden's death, Bill's right to rule the Hollow remained unchallenged.

Boyd Sullivan, youngest son of Wild Bill

[10] *Ibid.*

The Condemned

ALTHOUGH BILL'S REPUTATION was widely known in Sullivan's Hollow and throughout the state by the turn of the century,
so much tragedy occurred in the lives of Wild Bill and members of
his family in 1903 that a less stout-hearted man would not have
survived the year. It was this year that in later life Bill chose not to
include in interviews with newspapermen. In that year, he was
accused of murdering his own brother. In addition, one of Bill's
sons was involved even more deeply, and nine months later he
killed himself. In that same year, another of Bill's sons was murdered in the Hollow, and his eldest son was indicted for assault
with intent to kill. Nevertheless, Bill, then fifty-two, weathered
that tragic year; in fact, the sadness occasioned by these events
possibly caused Wild Bill to modify his reckless style of living.

This tragic year began with the murder of Bill's brother, Wilson W.
Sullivan, on January 31, 1903. Wilson was born April 3, 1862, and
married Josephine Keyes, a cousin of Bill's wife, Juriah. Wilson and
Josephine lived in the Hollow about a mile from Bill and Juriah. On
the night of the murder, Wilson and Josephine gave a candy breaking
for their relatives.[1]

A number of relatives and neighbors came to the party, and much

---

[1]Trial Transcript of Stenographer's Notes, *State of Mississippi vs. W. C. Sullivan*,
1903, p. 9. Candy breakings were a form of social activity for this era. Cane syrup was
boiled until it was thick enough to handle with the hands, whereupon two people
"pulled" the candy into long, thin threads. As it cooled, it would break, hence the
name "candy breaking."

drinking ensued. As the party was breaking up, Wilson left his home and went up the road a few hundred feet. Bill and his son Andrew Jack followed Wilson and a fight broke out. Wilson died as a result of knife wounds received in the fight. The courts indicted both Bill and Jack for the murder but Jack never stood trial. He hid out in the woods, and in the fall of 1903, he accidentally killed himself. Bill was found guilty by the Smith County Court but an appeal to the state supreme court freed him.

What really happened that fateful night has been the subject of continued argument. The original records of the court proceedings in the county seat of Raleigh were destroyed when the courthouse burned in 1912. However, since Wild Bill appealed his case to the supreme court, the transcripts of the trial at Raleigh, together with the briefs prepared for the court by both attorneys for the appeal case, are extant.

Court records reveal that Juriah did not attend the candy breaking, possibly because her youngest child, Boyd, was quite young. However, Bill went to the party, as did his fifteen-year-old daughter Myrtle, his twenty-year-old son Bobbie, and his son Andrew Jack, who by now had a family of his own. Jack's wife Altimare "Alice" Sullivan, daughter of Wiley P. (Big Wiley) Sullivan and Annie Terrissa Reddock, did not attend, for she and Jack had three small children, Volus, Eunice and Bonnie, all younger than six years old.

At the party were others who later testified at Bill's trial: Alex and Sam Spell, sons of Mary Ann Sullivan and third cousins of Wilson and Bill; Wilson's two sons—Lon, the eldest, and Rob, eighteen; Bob Sullivan, a nephew of both Wilson and Bill (their brother, Neece, had a son Robert Joshua, aged thirty-three at this time, so it could have been he); Hanz Sullivan (probably Hense); Luther B. Hopkins; Professor Hatton; Nob Dickinson, possibly a relative of Sam Spell's wife, who came with Alex Spell; and a black man named George Sullivan who worked for Wilson. Doubtless other people were present, but only these are mentioned in the transcript of the trial.

The state's chief witness, Josephine Keyes Sullivan, testified that her husband Wilson drank one dram before sundown with Mr. Hatton, although others testified that Wilson had consumed more. Wilson was said to be the type who got fussy when he had had only a few drinks. Josephine said Bill was drinking by the time he came to her house, and others stated that he was apparently drunk by the time he left the party. Most witnesses conceded that Wild Bill was loud and profane when he drank and, since he was loud and profane at the party, that he must have been drunk.

However, there apparently had been no arguments at the party. The court prosecutor did try to establish that there had been differences between the two brothers and their families, but even Josephine, who brought the charges against Bill, said that they were friendly at the time. Bill said that at the party he and his brother had lain across the bed, talking most of the time. In 1903 in rural Smith County, few houses had a room, except the kitchen, without a bed, therefore, reclining in the bed was perfectly natural.

At the trial, Hopkins's testimony reinforced the statements that Wilson and Bill had been drinking. He told of this incident which happened at the candy breaking.

> When I was in the room with Bill and Jack and Bobby and Wilson Sullivan, and Sam Spell, they were in there, and they had a bottle of whiskey. Jack or Bobby said to me, "take this and drink it up; old man Bill has got enough." Bill said, "Yes, drink it up." I taken a little swallow of it, and they taken the balance of it. They offered it back to me, and I said I did not want any of it. Bill spoke and says that he did not have but 10 or 15 cents and ran his hand in his pocket and pulled out two or three silver dollars and says, "Where did I get that?" I spoke; and Wilson spoke, he got it out of his pocket; he (Wilson) hit Bill on his shoulders with his hand and said he got it out of his pocket. I told him to put it back in his pocket, and he put it back in his pocket. He says to Wilson, "You don't want me in your house." Wilson says, "Yes, I am glad you came, and would be glad to have you stay all night." Bill says, "I won't let my girl go in any house of the settlement but yours." I spoke to him, "Yes, you would let her come in my house." Bill says, "Yes, I would," and they got him out in the dining room, then to supper, and that is all I heard.[2]

Josephine swore that at the party Bill had made a remark that he would get Wilson. She testified that Bill and Jack came in the front gallery, and Bill was calling for Wilson. She stated that she was standing in the hall and that Bill said, "Wilson is in here and I am going to have him." Her testimony stated further that Jack did not enter the house with his father. Upon being told that Wilson was not in the house, Bill went back out on the gallery and said, "By God, I

[2] *Ibid.*, 29–30.

am going to have Wilson before morning." Josephine said that Jack then took his father by the arm, saying, "Come on, Pa, let's go. We will find him."[3]

Wilson's oldest son, Lon, did not see the fight but reported that Bill and his father had been at outs, had had one or two fights, but were friendly at that time. He testified that he and Henz had started down to put up Henz's mule when he heard Bill say, "They have gone; let's go." He said that Bill and whomever he was talking to had just walked out in the yard from the gallery.

Josephine said Wilson had stepped out with Alex Spell. Alex, in testifying, stated that he had gone to Wilson Sullivan's that night after his brother. After he found Sam, they left for home. While walking along the road, Alex saw Wilson walking ahead of them. Wilson asked Sam, "Whereabouts is that stuff?" Sam answered that it was right upon the hill. Alex then heard somebody holler, and Bill came up and inquired, "Alex is that you?" Upon being told that it was, Bill answered saying, "Goddamn hell fire." Alex further testified that Wilson, who was standing near the side of the road, came up to Bill and said, "Bill, what do you mean?" Bill answered that he did not mean anything. Bill turned to walk off, whereupon Wilson said, "You ain't going." Alex reported that Wilson then said, "Bill, you have been throwing off on me and my folks all night and you are a Goddamn liar." About that time Wilson walked up to Bill's mule, and the mule jumped back.[4]

Alex and Sam and Nob left the scene but the noise of the fight was heard by those back at the house. Josephine said to the others: "I told them, 'if you all be silent, we can hear them fighting, cursing, and hear the licks to the house,' and I told them if they would hush, and that if Wilson was there, when he speaks, I can tell it, and Mr. Hopkins says 'He is out over there. I think that is him talking over there.' But it was not him over there [near the house]." Josephine added that she knew it was Bill's voice, that she would know it anywhere, for she heard him curse so much. A few minutes later George Sullivan, the black hired man, came up the road and said to Josephine's son Rob, "Run here, your Pa is all cut to pieces." George told the court that Jack and he were standing at the corner of the yard when Bill left

[3]Ibid., 10.
[4]Ibid., 57–58.

on his mule at a lope. Hearing a racket down the road, Jack had said that he was going over there with his keen cutter and settle it. George saw Wilson knock Bill down, and then Jack and Wilson fought. As George was going back to the house after the boys, he saw Bill act like he hit Wilson twice in the back.[5]

Next, Charlie Sullivan, a cousin of both Wilson and Bill, gave his testimony. When he had heard the noises of the fighting, he had rushed to observe it. Charlie got there before Rob did and he testified that he did not see anything in Bill's hand. He saw Wilson shove Bill down, and Bill get up and strike Wilson. Charlie swore that Bill was facing Wilson when Rob came up. Rob struck Bill with a four-foot picket, but Jack was standing close to Bill, off to one side, and he caught Rob's lick. Charlie confirmed that George Sullivan was standing nearby holding a gray mule. He concluded his testimony by stating that Jack took Bill by the arm, and they walked off in the old field.[6]

Rob Sullivan's testimony differed substantially from that given by either George or Charlie. He said he had a lamp, with a piece of timber in his other hand. He admitted that he struck at Bill, but Jack ran around and knocked the lick off. Rob further maintained that his father turned around and said, "They have killed me but did not scare me." Rob also swore that Wilson said to Bill, "You are cutting on me, too, Bill." When Jack took Bill by the arm and said "Let's go," Rob stated that Wilson turned around, sat down, and said, "Jack has killed me," and that his father died with his head in Rob's lap.[7]

About this time during the fray Josephine reached the scene. To the court, she reported that by the time she got to her husband he was almost dead, for he could not and did not speak. She assumed, therefore, that he had lapsed into a coma. She testified that when she got to Wilson "a darkey" was holding him up, and that Wilson had his feet under him and looked faint. He lived only a few minutes longer, and she told that Rob and George then carried Wilson's body to the house.

In his testimony Luther Hopkins said he stripped Wilson after the body had been brought to the house and that Wilson bled heavily

[5]*Ibid.*, 23, 66–68.
[6]*Ibid.*, 48–51.
[7]*Ibid.*, 33–34.

while being washed. Hopkins described Wilson's wounds by demonstrating their position on a model in the courtroom. (Later, lawyers for the supreme court noted that the position of the wounds should have been described accurately.) Hopkins stated that he intended to examine the body for wounds but he forgot to do that. However, later he did examine the top shirt worn by the victim and testified that there were five holes in it. When Hopkins continued to undress Wilson, he found a pocket knife, a pipe, and some tobacco. During cross-examination, Hopkins testified that one of the wounds was under the left shoulder blade and that to him it looked like a stab about as wide as a knife blade, as though a knife had been stuck in and pulled out.

Then Lon, Wilson's other son, testified that he also had gone to the site of the fight, getting there a minute or two after Rob. He said his father was already dead when he got there. He reported that he returned to the house before his father's body was brought there.

The record shows that Josephine took her husband's bloody shirts and had them washed. At the time of the original circuit court trial, in September, 1904, these shirts were still in her possession, although they had been exhibited at the grand jury hearing. Josephine also had Bill's hat which came off during the fight. In this trial, the defense attorney tried to get her to admit that there was only one knife hole in the back of the shirt whereas now there were three holes. She maintained, however, they were exactly as they were when they were taken off Wilson's body.

After the fight, a curious discovery was made. About fifty yards away from where the fight took place, Bill's mule was found shot. Several testified that they heard the gunblast, and several saw the mule dead on Sunday, the next day. As Alex Spell was testifying for the defense, the state attorney tried to refute his remarks about Bill's mule jumping back when Wilson called Bill a "Goddamn liar." To break the witness, the attorney asked sarcastically if it was the offensive language that the mule could not stand, or if the mule accepted Bill's remark of "Goddamn, hell fire." Alex remained cool and merely replied he did not know about that.

Later on Saturday night, Bob Sullivan, nephew of Bill and Wilson, went to Bill's house. He said that Bill told him about having a fight with Wilson but insisted that he had not gone to his brother's house for any fuss. Bill kept repeating that Wilson was as good a friend as he had, but that Wilson had come on to him for a fuss after he started home. At this point, Bill did not know that Wilson had died. Bob stated to the jury that Jack had had a knife that night but that Bill had taken it away from him. Bill told his son, "I will take the blame. You need not be scared."[8] Bill then shut the knife and put it in his pocket.

Although it does not clear up the mystery of who killed Wilson, Bill's own testimony may be more effective:

> Wilson had a candy breaking and ask me to come down. Me and him drank that night and stayed together most of the time. Lay on the bed nearly all the time. When I started home, we went out on the gallery there, and we talked awhile and I told him we all had a big time and I was going to see what my wife had to say about staying out so late. I went and got my mule and started, and when I got a piece from the house, I saw my brother, Wilson, and Sam Spell and Alex Spell, and I rode up there and hollowed, and Wilson asked me what I meant, and I told him I did not mean anything. He says, "Yes you have been throwing off on me all night." I said, "Wilson, I think more of you than any brother I got!" I said this, and Wilson started back to where his crowd was, and said I was a damn liar, and walked up to me and struck at me on the mule, and the mule throwed me; about that time, my son ran up there, and Wilson walked up and commenced to cursing at Jack, asked what did he have to do with it. I told him I did not come to have any fuss here, there is no use for it. When I said that somebody ran up and hit me with something. I don't know what it was. I thought more of my brother and stayed more with him and he was better to me than any of the balance of them, until he would get whiskey in him; he would quarrel then. I would not have been accused of such a thing for anything in the world. I never had anything to bother me like that did, my brother killed and me accused of it. Anyway, Jack he come to me and says, "come on" and I started with him and got ten to fifteen steps, and I told him to let me go back and get my mule. Jack says, "No, come on and go with me. I have cut Wilson, and they will kill you if you go back there," so we went on home.[9]

Bill testified that he may have hit Wilson, but he had used only his fists. He said that he and Jack spent the night at his house, and he did not hear that Wilson was dead until Sunday. He remained at home on Monday because he had heard that he and Jack were to be arrested. Jack left about one o'clock and no one knew where he had gone. On Tuesday morning, Bill went to a store that he operated at

[8] *Ibid.*, 53.
[9] *Ibid.*, 75–77.

Abel, west of Mize. He told Juriah to send for him or to tell the sheriff where he was. The sheriff came that evening, and sent a deputy sheriff, N. B. Boykin, for Bill. Jack followed the custom of evading arrest by hiding out in the woods surrounding the Hollow. As usual, many knew where he was, but their fierce loyalty prevented his being reported to the law.

Early in February, Wild Bill and the Spell brothers made two trips to see Justice of the Peace A. L. Jones at nearby Waco for a preliminary trial hearing. However, because of high water the witnesses could not appear, so trial was postponed. On Friday, February 25, 1903, W. C. Sullivan was bound over in bond of $2,000. Joe Rutledge, a farmer between Mize and Mt. Olive, was his bondsman. Charges against the Spell brothers were dismissed.

The grand jury returned a true bill against Jack and Bill in March, 1903. Jack was indicted along with Wild Bill but was not present as he was still in hiding. Brance Boykin and Walter Allen went to Bill's home and brought him to the Raleigh jail. Bill petitioned for a habeus corpus trial before Stone Devours, judge of chancery court, Smith County. This trial was held March 25, 1903, and Bill was granted additional bond of $3,000 until his case could be tried in circuit court. However, Bill's lawyers were successful in getting a continuance in every term. Before the trial was finally held in Raleigh, Jack had accidentally killed himself.

Judge J. R. Enoch presided over the case (#1148) in the Raleigh Circuit Court in September, 1904. He opened the court with a prayer by a minister, J. D. Crimes. The jury was composed of N. C. Wade, J. B. Hand, W. C. Traweeck, J. W. Cox, T. L. McRee, L. B. Edwards, R. H. Hester, W. H. Alexander, G. S. Davis, R. W. Bailey, C. E. Lee, and R. A. Grant. Their verdict read, "We the jury find the defendant guilty as charged in the indictment, and fix his punishment at imprisonment in the penitentiary for life." A neighboring county newspaper approved the verdict by writing that it would rid the county of one of its most immoral characters.[10]

On September 17, 1904, the defense filed a motion to set aside the verdict and asked for a new trial. The defendant was allowed ninety days in which to prepare and file a bill of exception. He appeared before the court and swore that he was a citizen of the state of Mis-

[10]"Smith County Circuit Court," *Simpson County News*, September 29, 1904.

sissippi but because of his poverty he was unable to pay the costs or deposit security necessary for an appeal to the state supreme court. He therefore asked the court to provide an appeal as provided by the law. The form was signed by the clerk, H. W. Tullos, with Bill's mark affixed.

Bill was ordered to be removed by the sheriff of Smith County to the jail of Hinds County in Jackson and to remain there until the supreme court heard his appeal. Mississippi law allowed convicted felons to go to the penitentiary, pending appeals to the supreme court, and the time thus served to count on their sentence in case of affirmation by the higher tribunal. The prisoner willingly accepted this and stated that work on the Rankin County convict farm was far more preferable to being confined in prison.

The *Clarion-Ledger* reported that Bill did not seem to be worried, that he believed that he would be acquitted and that his only source of uneasiness seemed to be the discomfort of the women and children left in the Hollow. The paper further reported, "The transfer to convict gallows brings an effectual close on one of the deadliest and most picturesque feuds in the history of the state. During the last twenty years, Sullivan's Hollow feuds have been responsible for the death of no less than forty people, all of the killings occurring in a little neighborhood in Smith County not over ten miles square. In its number of victims, the feud has far exceeded the celebrated Hatfield-McCoy affair of Kentucky."[11]

The Mississippi Supreme Court convened on November 14, 1904, with Chief Justice A. H. Whitfield presiding, and with assistance by Associate Justices S. S. Calhoun and Jeff Truly. The W. C. Sullivan case (#11368) was called for Monday, January 16, 1905. Sullivan was represented by D. A. McIntosh of Collins and W. H. Hughes of Raleigh. Assistant Attorney General J. N. Flowers delivered the argument for the prosecution.

The defense alleged that there were errors in the instructions to the jury given by the court in Raleigh. It cited the fact that no clear evidence was ever presented that Bill had a knife on the night of the murder. The defense also argued that the lower court had erred when it continued Jack's name on the indictment (Jack having died in September, 1903). The defense also pointed out that in the earlier trial

[11]*Jackson Daily Clarion-Ledger,* March, 1903.

three of the jury were impaneled without being sworn, and then only after Mrs. Josephine Sullivan had begun her testimony; neither had the court formally arraigned the prisoner until that time. Later, Judge Whitfield was to reprimand the lower court for these unlawful proceedings. Bill's case was finally heard on February 27, 1905, and the lower court decision was reversed and remanded, which was tantamount to Bill's being set free.

Bill's youngest son, Boyd, said his father returned to his home in Smith County, and no further trial was ever held. Unfortunately, the aftermath has led over the years to many distortions of the truth. Much sensationalism has consistently characterized stories told about the fratricidal conflict. Most probably the killing was the impulsive act of a man who had consumed too much whiskey. It was truly regretted by the defendant. However, since the case was never fully resolved, it reinforced the idea that Sullivan's Hollow was a place of lawlessness and that Wild Bill could do whatever he wished without punishment.

Ed Sullivan, son-in-law of Wild Bill and grandson of Thomas, with his son Hines (circa 1930)

The Sons

BEING ACCUSED OF THE MURDER of his brother Wilson was traumatic for Bill. But he experienced additional tragedy in 1903; three of his sons were involved in violence that resulted in the death of two of them.

On June 20, Julius Sullivan, eldest son of Wild Bill and Juriah, and Julius's brother Bobbie had gone by train from Abel, near Mize, to the county seat of Taylorsville. On the returning train was a young man, described as about twenty years of age, of medium size, with a rather handsome face, cold, steel eyes, and an erect bearing. People in the Hollow referred to him as Gus Adams; newspapers reported his name as R. O. Adams or R. J. Adams. He had lived in Smith County about two years and worked at the Anderson sawmill at Bunker Hill.

For some weeks Bobbie Sullivan and Adams both had been dating Beulah King. She lived near Bunker Hill, a flagstop on the Gulf and Ship Island Railroad. On several occasions, Bobbie had threatened to kill Adams if he did not stop his visits to the young lady; however, Adams disregarded the threats and continued his attentions to her. When the train reached Bunker Hill, Bobbie got off on one side of the coach, and Adams got off on the opposite side and across the tracks. Julius stayed on the train, continuing his trip to Abel. As the train pulled out of the Bunker Hill station, Bobbie stood near the depot with his hands up near his chest, as if in the act of cleaning his fingernails.

Adams stated to the police afterwards that Bobbie Sullivan called to him and said the trouble might as well begin. Adams replied that he thought so too. Adams said Sullivan ran his hand into his shirt to get his gun. Adams had his gun up his sleeve, and as he told a reporter, "I was the quickest. Before he could get his gun out, I shot him five times, once while he was standing, and three times while he was falling, and once on the ground."[1]

One of Julius's sons told what happened next:

> On that Saturday night about dark, someone passed Pa's house. He was sitting on his front porch, and they told Pa about Bobbie being shot by Adams. Pa didn't say a word, just got up and hitched his horse to the wagon. He went to Adams's house and when he got close, he called to Adams, saying, "I heared you got my brother dead under your front porch. I ain't carrying 'nary gun, but I'm coming on up there after my brother." Adams saw Pa wasn't armed, so he let him come on up and get Bobbie out from under the front porch, and then they buried Bobbie in the Zion Hill Cemetery.[2]

Adams was arrested, and was taken to Jackson on Sunday, June 21, and confined in the city jail for safe-keeping since Sheriff Martin of Smith County reported signs of discontent among the Sullivans. There were indications, he thought, that the Sullivans might at any time make an attack upon Adams to avenge the murder of their kin. Adams confessed that he had killed Bobbie, but he maintained that he acted in self-defense. Since Bobbie did not survive the shooting, there is only Adams's account to rely upon.

During the last week in September, Adams was brought back to Raleigh. Since no witnesses appeared before the grand jury, it failed to give the case a thorough investigation. Adams was taken back to Jackson to remain in custody until the next term of court.

On Saturday, October 3, 1903, Adams and two other prisoners escaped from the Jackson city jail. The *Clarion-Ledger* noted that Adams was in jail for the killing of Bud Sullivan, but since the grand jury had failed to indict him he would have been released in a few days. All three men who escaped had been confined in a cell on the north side of the jail. They succeeded in twisting the nuts from the bolts holding a metal patch in the cage door. They made an opening

---

[1]"Says He Did It," *Jackson Daily News*, June 22, 1903, p. 1; see also "Young Adams Tells Why He Killed Bobbie Sullivan," *Smith County Reformer*, July 2, 1903.
[2]Interview, Shep Sullivan, 1977.

large enough for them to crawl through to the corridor. From there they went to an assembly room which had a fireplace. Using hoops from a beer keg that had been in their cell as a stool, they dug out the brick in the fireplace chimney, and from knotted blankets made a rope which let them down from the second story into the yard. There was some evidence of help from the outside, for the imprint of a ladder beside the fence was discovered. The jailer estimated that they had escaped between one and four o'clock in the morning. No one saw them leave. On October 7, the jailer resigned. On October 8, one of the three escaped prisoners, Paul Gilmore, was captured in Vicksburg and brought back to Jackson. He said there had been no help from outside, and that once they had escaped, the men separated. Gilmore swore he did not know where Adams had gone.

Adams, however, could be traced. Another of Julius Sullivan's sons finished this story:

> Adams went back to Smith County around Saratoga. Dr. Harper from Laurel, and my grandad, Wild Bill Sullivan, had a store in Abel, about two miles from Mize. One day grandad was sitting in front of the store, on a bench of some sort there, and he saw a man coming down the tracks which ran in front of the store. He said "That man there looks like Adams who shot Bobbie." My pa was there and he said that it couldn't be, fer Adams was supposed to be in the Jackson jail. They set there a spell, then grandad got up, closed the store, and they went off somewhere. Later, we found out that they had gone out towards Saratoga, about nine miles from Mize. A friend of both my dad and grandad's sent my grandmother Juriah word saying that she would not have to worry about Adams anymore, for he was under the sawdust.[3]

Adams's body was later found in a sawdust pile. Some sources say he was killed by Bill and his brother Red Jack in Milton, a flagstop two miles west of Abel on the Gulf and Ship Island Railroad. Charges were never brought against the Sullivans because no evidence could be found.

Meanwhile, in September, 1903, Wild Bill's son Andrew Jack, known as Black Jack to distinguish him from his uncle Red Jack, was still in hiding because of his involvement in the murder of Wilson Sullivan. Jack, his brother Julius, and a few other men had met late Saturday night, September 26, at the depot in the town of Abel. Jack carried a Winchester rifle and wore a pistol in his belt around the

[3]Interview, Milton C. Sullivan, Jackson, Mississippi, 1977.

waist. He had laid his rifle on the depot platform. When he stooped down to pick it up, his pistol fell from the belt. The hammer of the pistol struck the Winchester and caused the pistol to discharge into his chest. He died a short time later.

Reactions varied widely concerning Jack's death. One account says that as he was dying Jack prayed to God for mercy and asked those present to pray also. Another account intimates that, although he died early Saturday night, his body was not discovered until Sunday morning. There seems to be general agreement that he killed himself accidentally since "from the man's disposition and his life, the shooting was certainly accidental as Jack Sullivan was a good fellow, and never brooded over his troubles."[4] However, another newspaper editor saw the issue somewhat differently for his heading read, "Black Jack Sullivan Is a Terror to the Hollow No Longer."[5] When Jack died, he left a widow, Alice, and five children, Volus, Eunice, Bonnie, Andrew Jack, Jr., and Emma.

Wild Bill's oldest son was Julius Evander (1871–1951) whose first wife was Sarah Elizabeth Ates (1868–1914). She was a daughter of John Ates and Mary Crockrell. John's mother was Frances Ates, who was married to a full-blooded Choctaw named Langford.[6] According to custom, children born to an Indian-white marriage carried the surname of their mother. Frances Ates appears in the 1850 Covington County census as a forty-five-year-old female (birthdate circa 1805) and gives her birthplace as Louisiana. By 1903, Julius and Sarah Sullivan had daughters Carrie (born 1892), Eula (1896), and a son Milton (1894). Two other sons, Harvey and Vernie, had died.

Julius also had trouble with the law in that fateful year, 1903, and the same judge that sent Bill to the Jackson jail sent Julius there. In fact, one headline noted "Father and Son in Stripes." There is no record in the state supreme court archives that Julius appealed his conviction. Julius admitted killing a man named Erle but maintained that he acted in self-defense. There were six indictments against him, but he pled guilty to a charge of assault and battery with

---

[4]"Jack Sullivan Killed," *Laurel Chronicle*, September 30, 1903.

[5]*Smith County Reformer*, October 1, 1903.

[6]Interview, Hulon Ates, Mize, Mississippi, 1977. Further research at finding the husband of Frances Ates proved futile. Oral accounts always maintained that she did have these children by a Choctaw Indian husband. An existing photograph supports this thesis.

intent to kill and was sentenced on this charge. The judge sentenced Julius to the penitentiary but gave him the option of serving his time working on the Rankin County Farm, which he accepted. The other five indictments were not processed.[7]

An almost humorous incident is told about one of the charges against Julius. Wild Bill, Julius, Sam Sullivan, and Dr. Harper had a store in Abel. Sam also ran the post office. Julius sold farmers a lot of fertilizer on credit. The farmers had a bad year, so Julius could not collect his debts. Julius had also sold bootleg whiskey to the farmers. He couldn't force them to pay for the fertilizer because if he did report them to the law, they would tell about his selling illegal whiskey.

Paul Byrd and John Wesley Gentry operated a store across the street from the Sullivans' store. The Byrds were long-time residents of the Hollow. Paul's father, Allen, had come there by 1850 from North Carolina. They were interrelated with the Sullivans insomuch as Allen Byrd had married Thomas Sullivan's daughter Caroline. Furthermore, Paul's sister Ellen had married John Wesley Gentry. The Byrds were very influential in the community and were rivals of the Sullivans in the mercantile business.

Therefore, the Sullivans were envious when Byrd obtained a cash register with a bell that rang so loudly that it could be heard across the road. Customers from far away came to the Byrd store to hear the bell as Byrd rang up the sale. The more the Sullivans saw their customers enter Byrd's store, the more they heard the ring of the cash register, the madder they got. In their anger they turned to whiskey.

One night after dark Julius, armed with a two-by-four, crossed the road, kicked down the door of the Byrd's store, destroyed the showcases, and attacked the bell. When the owner tried to interfere, Sullivan attacked the owner. The authorities indicted him for assault and battery with intent to kill.[8]

Julius continued his misdeeds in the county for some years. His daughter Eula always detested whiskey and she attributed her father's recklessness to his love of drink. To card playing, she also was stubbornly, unreasonably opposed. Julius, however, outlived his misdeeds, and in later life became an ardent church-goer. He was

[7]"Noted Feudists on Convict Farm," *Laurel Chronicle,* October 1, 1904.
[8]Interview, M. C. Sullivan, 1977.

a very good farmer, was generous to his neighbors, and was noted for growing fine cantaloupes and watermelons. Julius had seven children by his first wife, Elizabeth Ates, two of whom are still living; he had six children by his second wife, Mary Etta Wallace, of whom four are living. Julius lived to be seventy-five, confirming the legend that if a Sullivan outlived the escapades of his earlier years he lived an unusually long life.

Wild Bill's other son, Boyd (1894–1978) left Smith County and served in World War I in France. He also worked for a railroad in Chicago for many years. Like Wild Bill, he had a twinkle in his eye that showed his sense of humor, especially as he related war stories or revealed that bending the elbow at bars had cost him his railroad job. Boyd lived in California for some years before returning to Mississippi.

The events concerning his sons were upsetting to Bill but did not defeat him. After winning his appeal to the supreme court in 1904, Bill returned to Smith County where he lived until his death in 1932.

During his final years, Bill left his farmhouse and moved near Mize. He joined the Baptist Church and became an exemplary citizen. He even gave up strong drink entirely, and after Mississippi voted to be dry he was instrumental, it is said, in the arrest of several bootleggers.

After giving up farming, Bill became an itinerant salesman. He traveled over Smith and Covington counties in his buggy, selling salve, flavoring, and buttons. Being well acquainted with everyone for miles around, he would spend the night with whomever he was with when nighttime came. His stories and tales became legendary, but he rarely mentioned the killings he was involved in. Many of his grandchildren never heard him mention the violence, but knew their grandfather instead as a recounter of stories and a man who liked jokes. He loved children and enjoyed bouncing a child on his knee as he sang an old-time ditty.

Wild Bill lived to eighty-two, and his health remained good until the last few weeks of his life. He died Sunday, June 26, 1932, at the home of his daughter Martha Ann and his son-in-law Thomas Pickering. On the day before he died, his granddaughter, Eula Sullivan Howell, and her seven children came by to see him. He lay motionless on the bed in the front room. He was incoherent and his death rattle had begun. On the back porch, with her hands folded in her lap, sat Juriah, calmly awaiting his end. Reports say she waited with the same serenity and trust that she had awaited his return from his many nights out.

At his death, though he had been out of the spotlight for twenty-five years, he was still widely remembered. One newspaper reported his death thus:

"King of the Hollow" Dead
Wild Bill Sullivan Dies at 81
Colorful Career Ended

Death of Wild Bill removed one of Mississippi's most colorful figures whose career in the Smith County empire labeled him variously as outlaw, fugitive, and good citizen. In recent years, Bill's life has been quiet and staid, though he always enjoyed reminiscences of the old days. He is survived by a brother, Henry of Mize, two sons, Julius of Mize, and Boyd of Chicago; and three daughters, Mrs. H. S. Bryant, Mize, Mrs. Joe Sullivan, Mize, and Mrs. Tom Pickering, Mt. Olive, Ms.[9]

In the *Smith County Reformer*, the local newspaper, the editor both commended Wild Bill and dismissed his checkered past:

A noted landmark was removed from Smith County last Sunday when the spirit of W. C. (Bill) Sullivan bade farewell to the form that had been its habitat for more than eighty years and winged its flight to realms eternal. Mr. Sullivan was perhaps the most picturesque character connected with that section of Smith County known as Sullivan's Hollow, and the stories concerning which have often been exaggerated to the hurt of many of the best and bravest that Smith County has ever produced. He possessed many noble traits. Let's forget his faults as we drop the last bouquet of respect on his grave.[10]

By 1977, a young minister in preaching the funeral of Wild Bill's grandson Cranford, who like Bill was inclined toward strong drink, summed up the Wild Bill character: "Mr. Sullivan had a problem. We all have problems; it is just that his problem was more evident to others than most of our problems are."[11]

Juriah survived her husband less than a year. She died suddenly on May 16, 1933. As one relative said, "She just dropped dead." One of

[9]*Jackson Daily News*, June 28, 1932, p. 1.
[10]*Smith County Reformer*, June 30, 1932, p. 1.
[11]Ricky Edwards, pastor, Oak Grove Baptist Church, July, 1977.

the grandsons gave his view of her passing: "When Grandpa Bill died, he had $200 [a considerable sum of cash in 1932] in a chest, but one of his daughters used it to open a store, and when Grandma died, it was the neighbors who made a pine casket to bury her in."[12] They buried her in Zion Hill Cemetery, next to her infamous husband.

Mack Sullivan and his wife Virginia, grandchildren of Thomas Sullivan

[12]Interview, M. C. Sullivan, 1977.

Virgil Marion Howell and Eula Sullivan Howell (granddaughter of Wild Bill). The Howells are descendants of Thomas Sullivan, and he is the author of an unpublished manuscript on Wild Bill.

PART THREE
The Twentieth Century
1900–1980

Dan Peter Sullivan, former sheriff of Smith County (1930)

Other
Smith County Stories

ALTHOUGH SMITH COUNTY is noted for the tales about Wild Bill, a group of the Sullivan stories center around Saratoga and Merry Hell, where Joseph Sullivan and his son Jeff lived. People in the Hollow say that this locality to the southwest of them was not a part of the Hollow. However, as the family multiplied, this area likewise was settled by Sullivans. Stories told about them are very similar to those tales told about the Sullivans in the older part of the Hollow, and thus they contributed to the Sullivan reputation and enhanced the Sullivan mystique.

One such escapade was recounted by Wild Bill, and it is known in the Hollow as the Little Bill McAlpin Affair.[1] It concerns four outlaws who organized a clan known as the Four Clingers, the leader of which was Little Bill McAlpin of Mize. Time and again there were mysteries, perhaps associated with them, that were never solved in Sullivan's Hollow. The Clingers were so closely allied that every shot they fired seemed to be noiseless and every track apparently covered. Their watchword was "Slow but Sure."

They had not been organized so very long when they decided to take in a fifth member, Jasper Thornton, who was a shrewd eighteen-year-old, very knowledgeable in the ways of Sullivan's Hollow. Before deciding to take Jasper in, the clan discussed his virtues from every angle; afterwards they decided he might strengthen their group. Jasper took the initiation oath that made him one of the

---

[1]The story told here is practically verbatim from Howell's ms.

Clingers. Then they called themselves the Five Clingers. Citizens often heard them singing, "Hail! Hail! The Gang's All Here." Seemingly, they terrorized the Hollow, but were able to successfully evade arrest. Moreover, opposition to the clan was minimal because citizens feared them.

About 1899 the group organized a raid in the course of which they lost confidence and trust in Jasper Thornton, but the other four Clingers were perplexed as to how to eliminate Jasper from their gang. At Harmony Church one Sunday during a protracted meeting, Little Bill McAlpin and Jasper Thornton, mounted on one horse, galloped northward in the direction of Cohay Swamp. About two hours passed, and Little Bill returned to church without Jasper. A night and almost a day had passed before Jasper's folks became concerned and wondered why he had not returned home from the Sunday's services. No one seemed to be overexcited at his prolonged absence because Jasper had often stayed away overnight without notifying his mother and father.

After two days and nights had passed, Little Bill visited Jasper's mother and father and informed them that Jasper had gone to Louisiana to visit one of his uncles. He also told Jasper's mother that he had bought Jasper's horse. This news was consoling to her. The next day she wrote Jasper a letter, but the uncle wrote back that Jasper had not been there. The family became excited. They could not believe that Jasper would leave home without telling them about his intentions. Their imaginations were running wild; they told their neighbors, the neighbors talked, conclusions were drawn, and the Clingers were suspected of foul play.

Both citizens and officers began to investigate, but not a trace of Jasper could be found. Finally a feeble old gentleman, too old to venture from his house to the protracted meeting on that Sunday, told that he had seen Little Bill and Jasper pass his house, go into the swamps, and shortly afterwards Little Bill had returned by himself. This information caused another old man to remember seeing Little Bill with a shovel on his shoulder in Cohay Swamp a day or two after the protracted meeting. Little Bill had told him that he was going down to the stream and ditch off a lake to catch fish. This information was enough; Little Bill was placed in jail and the swamp was searched. Days and nights passed by, but they could not find the body. Some gave up the search, but others were determined to find the body even if it took months. They were not going to overlook any square foot of the swamp, some of which was thicker than the African jungles.

Just after five o'clock on the twenty-ninth day of searching, W. Beavers of Mize was searching in the swamp about two hundred feet from a road. As he started to leave for the day, he noticed a small piece of clothing hanging to the thorn of a bamboo briar. He examined it and the ground nearby and he found a small bit of mud at the foot of a tree. When he raked the leaves, he discovered other bits of clothing. He called to other searchers. They found Jasper's grave and a badly decomposed body, which was identified as Jasper Thornton. The head had been cut off and tied up in a large handkerchief, and the body had been disfigured by knife wounds. The mutilated body was carried back to Harmony Church and buried.

The entire surrounding countryside was raging for revenge, but the Thornton family prevented the mobs from overpowering the law and taking the prisoner. The sentiment died down somewhat as time passed, and when Little Bill was tried, he asked for and obtained a change of venue to Jones County. He was found not guilty, because the evidence presented was all circumstantial.

After Little Bill was set free, he settled down. For several years he lived as quietly as anyone. He took life seriously and gained the confidence of the people of Sullivan's Hollow and the surrounding country.

One Saturday afternoon, October 24, 1903, Little Bill and a group of men came galloping up and down the main street of Mize. Little Bill was shooting a gun in each hand as he rode through town. Horses tied to the hitching posts became excited and broke loose. The owners preferred to stay indoors rather than endanger themselves by going out after their horses. The town now belonged to Little Bill, and no one was going to try to take it away from him; even the town marshall stayed in.

Near sundown Little Bill started riding homeward. Shortly after he left town, shots were heard that did not sound like Little Bill's guns. Everything now became quiet, and people ventured out. McAlpin had been shot at close range, with twenty-seven shots in his face, head, and neck. Word that he was dead soon spread around.

However, nothing was ever said or done about catching the killer. This type of frontier justice characterized the Hollow even into the twentieth century.

Another well-known episode, often incorrectly referred to by newspapers as the last of the violence in the Hollow, is known as the basketball affair. On February 24, 1922, the Magee High School basketball team from Simpson County was playing Smith County Agricultural High at Mize. Since the rivalry between these two neighboring towns was always keen, the atmosphere was tense and tempers flared easily. Basketball in 1922 in southern Mississippi was played on an open court, usually clay, hardened by years of use. Spectators sat on wooden tiers of benches, only two or three feet from the court. Some male spectators did not even take a seat during a game. Exchange of insults between supporters of both teams, between teams, or between spectators and officials was quite common. Moreover, the entire town population would show up for the game, since athletic events were the main social outlet for the community.

On this afternoon, more than three hundred persons attended the game. Although drinking, carrying weapons, and fighting were considered illegal, there were few men at the game without a drink or weapon. Given these circumstances, plus a close game ending in a squabble over a technicality which caused the referee to terminate the game, it is not surprising that the event resulted in the death of two citizens—one a Sullivan—and the wounding of three other persons.

When the referee ended the game, there was no sign of violence among the players or officials. The town marshall, Albert Lack, ordered everyone to stay off the court. When Warren Ashley entered the area and Marshall Lack tried to remove him, Ashley began firing a pistol at the officer. Judge Hughes of the Smith County Circuit Court was among the spectators. He seized Ashley in an effort to disarm him. However, Ashley, about thirty-five, was too vigorous to be restrained by a man over sixty. Ashley, who had been involved in previous difficulties, was the town barber and, when sober, was congenial and law-abiding. Yet on the day of the quarrel, Ashley was reported to have been drinking "blind-tiger" whiskey and to have been betting on the game. During the fracas with Judge Hughes, Ashley's wife clutched his arm trying to keep him out of trouble.

Meanwhile, Lack returned Ashley's fire and a stampede resulted. Ashley died within three minutes. His wife and Marshall Lack received wounds during the shooting.

About seventy-five yards away, Volus Sullivan was found dead, killed by a stray bullet. The thirty-year-old farmer was highly respected in the community. He had been the star of the local basketball team during his high school days, and was one of Smith County High's most avid supporters. His father was Andrew Jack (Black Jack), a son of Wild Bill Sullivan. Volus was married and the father of one child.

Dolpus Yelverton, a student from Taylorsville School, a few miles east of Mize, was wounded by a stray bullet. He had come to Mize to visit his cousins, Sallie and Bernice Yelverton. He was transported to a hospital in Laurel, but his wound was not critical.

The principals of the two schools, Professor S. H. McDonnell of Mize and Professor G. C. Hamilton of Magee, were present at the game. After the initial shock of the shooting had passed, Hamilton took his players home without giving them time to change uniforms.

Later that night the sheriffs of both counties served a warrant of arrest on Tullos Mangrum at his home in Magee. Tullos, the marshall of Magee, had been deputized by Marshall Lack of Mize to assist in the maintenance of order in the school contest. Tullos was charged with the killing of both Ashley and Sullivan.

J. L. Anderson, mayor of Mize, claimed that the bullets that had grazed Mrs. Ashley and had killed Ashley and Sullivan came from Mangrum's revolver. He further asserted that one of the Magee players, Frank Mangrum, had used insulting words to Mrs. Ashley, whereupon Ashley became infuriated and stormed out on the playing court area. Anderson said that another Magee player, Charlie Tullos, kicked Ashley in the stomach; he stated that several guns appeared in the Magee delegation, and the shooting became general.

Ben Frank Courtney, a student at Millsaps College, had helped to referee the game. He stated that the confusion prevented anyone from knowing clearly exactly what happened, but he thought that Ashley had come onto the court to tell Frank Mangrum to stop talking to some of the female spectators. Other spectators agreed with his report. Courtney left Mize with the Magee players.

Newspapers printed statements by Ashley's friends, who declared that he was not a drinking man. Also, a letter was sent to the *Daily Clarion Ledger* from E. B. Traylor, mayor of Magee, setting at rest any fears of an intercommunity war over the incident, offering deep sympathy to the families of Ashley and Sullivan, and expressing the good wishes for the complete recovery of Yelverton and Marshall Lack.[2]

Despite a hearing, nothing was done about the allegations because nobody knew for sure who shot whom. Once again, violence in the Hollow went unpunished.

The casualty of the fracas, Volus P. Sullivan, had only one brother, Andrew Jack Sullivan, Jr., who was also the victim of a killing. Their mother was Hattie Mae Wade whose father, George Wade, married Belle Sullivan. Andrew Jack married Myrtle Howell, daughter of Francis Craven and Alabama Mae Keyes Howell. Hillard Spell was a son of Sam Spell and was a greatgrandson of Thomas Sullivan. In the early spring of 1936, during a game of craps and a bout of drinking, Spell shot Andrew Jack. At the time of his death, Andrew Jack and his wife were parents of four children.

Near Saratoga another murder episode involved the Sullivans. Taylor, one of Wild Bill's nephews, was a veteran of the Spanish-American War. After the war, he became an employee of the Gulf and Ship Island Railroad. He was married to Della Wood, sister of Annie Jane Wood who had married W. M. Howell.

On Sunday morning, November 16, 1902, Taylor boarded the train at Saratoga and went to Laurel, but he did not return on the train that afternoon. When the train reached Saratoga, the postmaster, J. T. Robinson, and his brother-in-law, T. J. Walters, went through the cars searching for Sullivan. They were heard to say that they were going to kill him once they had found him. A short while after dark, gunshots were heard in the neighborhood of the depot. Sullivan was found dead with his brains shot out, and a hole in his right side where a load of buckshot had been emptied. His head was severed from his body, apparently by an ax. There were no eyewit-

---

[2]"Two Killed—Three Wounded in Mize Fight," *Jackson Daily Clarion-Ledger*, February 25, 1922, p. 1. Also, "Sheriff Arrests Tullos Mangrum in Mize Tragedy," *Jackson Daily Clarion-Ledger*, February 26, 1922, p. 1. Many newspapers later told of this incident, but erroneously gave the date as 1923 or 1924. Issues of local newspapers such as *Smith County Reformer* are unavailable for this story.

nesses to the shooting. However, a pistol which had been pawned by a man named Homer to T. J. Walters for some whiskey was found near the body.

The killing may have resulted from a family quarrel which involved questions about a woman's chastity. Grover Bishop said that T. J. Walters worked for the railroad company also, and that Taylor Sullivan had said something to Mrs. Walters that she did not like, so she told her husband whereupon he shot and killed Taylor.

After an inquest was held, Sheriff Magee of Simpson County arrested both Robinson and Walters, and on November 18, he took them to the Hinds County jail at Jackson. On November 19, the two prisoners were taken to Mendenhall, the seat of Simpson County, for arraignment. Several shots were fired as they got off the train. Consequently, the officers did not think that it was safe to let the prisoners stay in Mendenhall for fear of an impromptu rope-stretching party. The two prisoners also requested to be taken back to Jackson. On November 20, they were returned to Saratoga and were released on a bond of $1,000 until the next term of circuit court. Sylvester L. McIntosh and George W. May served as attorneys for the two men and the McIntosh brothers served as prosecutors in the case. Howell's history says Robinson was found guilty of this crime.[3]

Many acts of violence occurred at the sawmill at Bunker Hill. This sawmill, a sash mill, was first erected by Francis Marion Howell and Wiley Sullivan. At one time, when a man named Eaton attempted to kill his brother-in-law, Hathorn, to obtain possession of it, Eaton stabbed Hathorn three times in the back, and two shots were put through his chest by a man named Yawn who accompanied Eaton. While Eaton was stabbing him, Hathorn seized his own pistol and shot Eaton through the heart and killed him. Hathorn recovered from his wounds and lived eighteen years after this incident.

Robert Dean then got control of the sawmill. He dammed up Mill Creek and flooded several acres of land to provide power to run the mill. Dean was greatly disliked by many of his neighbors. Several of them lay in ambush waiting for a chance to shoot him. On May 11,

[3]For information on the Taylor Sullivan affair, see *Jackson Evening News*, November 17, 18, 20, 1902; *Simpson County News*, November 20, 27, 1902; *Laurel Chronicle*, November 18, 1902; and *Smith County Reformer*, November 27, 1902.

1899, they thought that chance had come. That night they saw a boat about a quarter of a mile out on Mill Creek pond. The men thought the occupant in the boat was Dean so someone fired a Winchester shotgun at him. However, George N. Sullivan, oldest son of Neece, was the person who had been killed.

Sam Sullivan (Thomas's son) and Mack and Vernon Howell (sons of F. M. Howell) were indicted by the court for the murder of George Sullivan. By 1901, two hearings had been held, but they both resulted in mistrials.[4] The case was finally tried in the March, 1903, circuit court at Raleigh. Bee Sullivan, son of Little Wylie, was a witness for the prosecution as was Victor Sullivan, sometimes called Bud or Bud Joe. Howell's history credits Sam Sullivan with the killing.

The two witnesses in the case, Bee and Bud Joe, are the central characters in another Sullivan episode. A group of the Sullivans and their relatives had a secret organization in which members could be compelled to participate in any activity voted on by the majority. Bee Sullivan thought that Bud Joe was going to reveal some details to the public about some horse thievery, so Bee shot Bud Joe. He was aided in the murder by Albert Sullivan, his brother-in-law. Bud Joe was found dead in the woods, with two bullet holes through his heart. Some say Bee made Ab shoot Bud Joe also so that Ab could not tell on him. When Bud Joe was found by Brown Lee, an infamous bully of Saratoga, Bud Joe's horse bridle was hanging around his shoulder.[5] Bee and Albert were tried, but as there were no witnesses, they could not be found guilty.

Ruby Huff, researcher for the Works Progress Administration in 1936 provided later facts:

> Bee went to Kansas City (some sources say St. Louis) leaving his wife and children to struggle as best as they could and to worry over his disappearance. The wife and mother was crushed at the blow, but held her head up, and worked hard to supply the wants of her dear orphaned children, fearing all the while that some ill luck had befallen her poor husband, despite the fact that neighbors rumored that he was off running around.
>
> The eldest boy grew to manhood and took over drudgering and the responsibilities of the home; yet he did it resentfully because he felt that a

[4]*Laurel Chronicle*, March 14, 1902, p. 6; also *Jackson Daily Clarion-Ledger*, March 11, 1903.
[5]Sullivan, *Sullivan's Hollow*, 79.

father should do his duty by his own. The only daughter grew up and was worshiped by her brothers because she was so beautiful, tender, kind and loving to them and their mother.

One day like a bolt out of the clear blue the father returned, much surprised to find a grown family and the lovely daughter. He had won a fortune while away, so he lavished his riches upon this beautiful daughter, gave her a car, fur coat, and tendered many other expensive gifts to her.

Naturally the sons resented this because they hated the father and his tainted money. They also hated the idea of having to lose the lovely sister; yet their resentment made the father more determined, so when he left, he slipped the girl off with him.

This enraged the oldest son, Newt, so he went after the sister and brought her back to the broken-hearted mother. Hardly had they returned, when the father had some of his relatives slip the girl to him again. The girl was so thrilled with the sudden luxury and the life of the big city, that she stayed against the wishes of her mother and family.

One day the son went to the city and waited his chance. When he saw the girl leave the apartment, he rushed in and shot his father.[6]

This killing occurred in 1938, and, shortly afterwards, Newt himself was slain in Laurel, but his assassin was never found.

Albert Sullivan was involved in yet another incident. Since he was a great-grandson of Thomas, grandson of Jefferson, and a son of Joseph, Albert was a lifelong resident of the Hollow. One of his neighbors, John Beavers, was afraid of Ab because Ab picked on him and ran over him. One day Ab was following his usual custom of tormenting Beavers, so Beavers shot and killed him. (This is the same Albert whose first wife, Minnie King, was accidently killed. Albert was helping Minnie with spring housecleaning when the bedsprings he was carrying accidentally dislodged the shotgun on the wall, whereup the gun fired, killing Minnie.) Ab's second wife, Ollie Sullivan, was Bee's sister, and since Bee had married Ab's sister, Ida, they were twice brothers-in-law.

Levi Sullivan was one of the twin boys born to Henry, Wild Bill's brother, and his wife, Mary Eubanks. Levi's twin brother was called Leon and was married to Beulah Blakeney. Levi never married, but he was courting a young lady in the Ely community. Levi was very boisterous and was overbearing, whereas Leon Bryant, a young man

[6]Ruby Huff, "Follow up Murder Stories," WPA Materials, Mississippi Department of Archives and History, June 22, 1936, p. 1.

who also claimed the young lady as his girl, was known to be fairly meek. Nevertheless, in 1917, at church on Sunday, Leon Bryant slew Levi with a cheap pocketknife. Leon was sentenced to a term in prison, but was pardoned by petition a few years later.

A few years after Levi's death, another Sullivan was killed in the Hollow. Tommie Sullivan was married to Mary Hall, whose brother Bud Hall had married Mary M. Sullivan, a daughter of Big John, son of Hog Tom, son of Thomas. Bud Hall was a larger man than Tommie, and on several occasions he provoked trouble with Tommie over something that Sullivan's wife or children did. On one occasion Hall made his wife whip Tommie's wife. Sullivan swore out a warrant against Hall and the court found him guilty of assault. Angry because of this conviction, Hall pulled a knife on Sullivan, whereupon the latter shot Hall with his shotgun. Sullivan was acquitted for the killing, but later Bud Hall's son shot Tommie.[7]

One of the wildest melees occurred just outside the Hollow on the way to the county seat of Raleigh. It occurred in 1903, that tragic year for the Sullivans. In reporting on this feud of February, 1903, the reporter said, "The committal of crime has reached an alarming point in Smith County, and in nearly ever case, mean liquor plays a conspicuous part."[8]

This fracas involved members of the Windham and Ainsworth families. Anse Windham had been legally accused by his sister-in-law, the daughter of A. L. (Coon) Ainsworth, of being the father of her illegitimate child. At the preliminary hearing, Judge Andrew Bryant bound Windham over with a bond of $1000 and ordered him to appear at the next session of the circuit court.

Upon hearing that Windham was to be released on bond, Coon Ainsworth kicked over the table, threw the justice docket out the door, and cursed the justice of the peace. He forbade any of the Windhams to go on the bond. Then he attacked Anse Windham personally, and the shooting erupted. Coon's two sons, Jesse and Stoney, took part in the fracas. Over one hundred gun and pistol shots were reported to have been fired in this melee. On the Windham side, Anse was assisted by his kinsmen, Bill, Ransom, and Ole Windham.

---

[7]*Ibid.*, also see Sullivan, *Sullivan's Hollow*, 63.
[8]"Bad Times in Smith," *Jackson Daily Clarion-Ledger*, March 11, 1903; *Smith County Reformer*, February 26, April 30, Mary 28, 1903.

Outside the courtroom, the battle continued with the Windhams pursuing the Ainsworths to their home in the southeastern part of Smith County.

Stoney Ainsworth was so severely wounded that he died about a week after the fray; Coon and Jesse were wounded and hospitalized, but they recovered. Anse Windham was wounded in the side. A mule and a dog were also killed. It is remarkable that no more damage was done in the midst of such an array of flying bullets.

W. W. (Bill), Ransom, and Ole were tried before Justice Sam Runnels. Bill was refused bail, but the other two Windhams were acquitted. Bill had his habeas corpus trial at Taylorsville on May 23, 1903, before Judge Deavors and was granted bail in the sum of $4,000.

The Ainsworths continued their acts of violence. Although little information is available on the case, one incident involved the murder of Harvey Stringer by Will Ainsworth. Supposedly this affair was caused by a rendezvous between Stringer and Ainsworth, whereupon an argument erupted. Stringer tried to evade the attack by fleeing in his car. After a sixty-mile chase, Ainsworth cornered Stringer near an old artesian well at Taylorsville and shot him.

That same year saw Mack Ingram charged with killing L. C. Little, the assessor of Smith County, over the possession of a little orphan girl. In March the grand jury returned a true bill of indictment for murder against Ingram. Also, Dewey Jack Sullivan killed George Smith in 1903. George Smith had come to the Hollow to work at the sawmill. He came from Ita Bena, Mississippi, and was a brother to Bennon Clark's wife who did live in the Hollow.[9]

The Sullivans' violent nature sometimes found an expression in a manner more acceptable to legalized established society—war. Information available on the Smith County Sullivans proves that they fought ably in the American Civil War.

The six youngest sons of Thomas Sullivan—Mark, Wiley, Sam, Conn, Loten, and Alex—and John Spell, who became their brother-in-law, served in various Confederate units. Mark enlisted July 22, 1863, as a private in Company C, 8th Mississippi Infantry under Captain Ward. Courtmartialed at Dalton, Georgia, for being AWOL, Mark was reprieved from death by his commanding officer, Captain

[9]*Simpson County News,* January 29, 1902.

George Buchanan, and was discharged from service when hostilities ended.

Wiley P. (Big Wiley) also served in the Confederate Army but little is known of his record. Samuel R. enrolled as a private in Company C, 8th Regiment, with Captain Wood, June 1, 1861, and was apparently injured or sick most of the time from October, 1862, until the end of the war.

Cornelius J. (Conn) enlisted in 1862. He was assigned to Company D, under Captain McGill in Colonel Boyles' 56th Alabama Regiment. After twelve months service with this outfit, he was transferred to Company B of the 46th Mississippi Regiment. He was a prisoner at one time. His command surrendered in 1865 at Blakely, Alabama. Conn's brother Loughton (Loten) also served with Company B, 46th Mississippi Infantry.

Alexander, Thomas Sullivan's youngest son, enlisted in June, 1862, when he was sixteen. He served for three years in Company B under Captain Jasper Eaton, with the George W. Stubbs batallion. His unit surrendered near Canton, Mississippi, but Alex was on pass at home to get a horse when the surrender occurred.

Thomas Sullivan had numerous grandsons who fought in the Civil War. Among them were Howells, Byrds, Harveys, Tews, Owens, Tuggles, Clarks, Gentrys, Bishops, and others, but only those with the Sullivan surname follow:

Daniel B. Sullivan, oldest son of Thomas (Hog Tom) and grandson of Thomas, served with Company F, 39th Infantry from 1862 until discharged at Durham, North Carolina, on April 26, 1865.

Another Daniel, son of Loderick, son of Thomas, served also in Captain Ward's 8th Infantry, but his service record is not available.

Stephen Sullivan, senior and junior, are recorded as privates in Company G of the 5th Infantry. Presumably, Stephen, Sr. (Tom's fifth son) enlisted August 23, 1862, and was mustered out at Columbus, Mississippi, September 22, 1863. According to family oral history, Stephen, Jr. served in his father's place and paid the supreme sacrifice in the Battle of Shiloh.

Thomas G. (Long Tom), son of Stephen and grandson of Thomas, enlisted July 30, 1861, under Captain W. T. Ward in Colonel Flint's 8th Infantry Regiment. Thomas was promoted to second lieutenant, but he resigned his rank on August 29, 1964, because of an unspecified disease and because of his limited knowledge of military tactics. His service record states that he testified at his courtmartial that he was unable to maintain healthy discipline, and thus his unit was inefficient. Being found guilty of negligence in battle, he was imprisoned by the Confederacy but was paroled at Meridian in 1865.

Another Stephen, son of Joseph, was killed during the Battle of Vicksburg. His brother, Orlando Jack, enlisted in 1864 and served under Captain Bill Vinzant in Ewall's Guard.

Thomas Jefferson Henderson Sullivan, son of Frederick, son of Thomas, enlisted in 1860, Company B, 46th Infantry Regiment, and served with Captain Magee under Colonel Easterling. Near the close of the war he was captured, but he was honorably discharged in 1865 from the federal prison at Ship Island.

His brother, John Wiley (Little Wiley), served the C.S.A. as a captain and, after his return to Mississippi, was elected to a two-year term, 1886–1887, in the Reconstruction legislature.

Sullivans also served in the Spanish-American conflict and World Wars I and II. Indeed, the service records of Thomas Sullivan's descendants show service in every branch of the military (Army, Navy, Marines, Air Force, Coast Guard, Women's Auxiliaries) and heroic action in countless battles throughout the global theaters of World War II.

Fifty Years
of Change

CHANGE HAS AFFECTED Sullivan's Hollow. Not all of it has been good. Much of the tradition which has made the Hollow unique has been altered. Many of the Sullivan traits that gave this family universal appeal have disappeared with modern progress and the move to urban areas, but those who treasure the Hollow for what its past was and for its meaning to early Mississippi history are sincerely pleased that the allure has not completely disappeared.

Howell's account of the Hollow describes religious and educational progress in the 1930s. What he describes may seem obsolete in the 1980s, but they are a basis for a comparison of the two eras.

The last ten or fifteen years have seen Sullivan's Hollow and Smith County making very rapid progress along religious and educational lines. There are, at present, about eighty-five churches in Smith County and of this number about fifteen are in or near Sullivan's Hollow. Every person in Sullivan's Hollow now has an opportunity to hear the Gospel preached as well as the people in any other community in Mississippi. During the summers, all the churches have protracted meetings from three days duration to ten days and great crowds of people attend daily, most of whom are Sullivans and they are who support the churches with money and spirit in the furtherance of our Lord's kingdom here. These people have much pride in the appearance of their churches and the church grounds, and do not refrain from contributions to their spiritual welfare. They are deeply interested in religion and still love "The Old Time Religion."

Since the year 1920 there have been several foreign missionaries to go out from Smith County. The town of Mize is proud of having sent two young women to the foreign fields. Miss Cavie Clark gave two years work to Brazil. Miss Myrtie Bryant who elected to go to Africa has been almost five years there. Sullivan's Hollow has given several of their worthy people to religious causes. Some of the most prominent preachers of Mississippi today are from Sullivan's Hollow and are proud of it. Thus, Sullivan's Hollow is contributing men and money to the cause of religion.

Few sections of the state can claim better school advantages than Sullivan's Hollow. Thirty-five schools for white children are operated in Smith County at present, six of which are affiliated schools. Sullivan's Hollow itself has one of the largest consolidated schools in the county to which most children of this section go. From this school, the graduates attend Smith County Agricultural High School at Mize, Mississippi, which is one of the largest in the state from which about fifty students graduate each year. The schools of Mize enroll each year around six hundred pupils. At Mize each year a summer normal for graded school teachers is held and is well attended and its efficiency is recommended by all. Here teachers renew licenses or do preparatory work to getting college degrees. We boast that Sullivan's Hollow has without a doubt sent more students to college all over the state than any other community of the same size in Mississippi. Smith County, more especially Sullivan's Hollow, has been noted for its champions and has always been a strong contender. Smith County has had more boys on college varsity teams at one time than any other county in the state. In 1923, with Mississippi A & M College, when it won Southern Championship, five of the eight players were from Mize. Since that time other colleges of the state have had Smith County boys on their teams and these players were outstanding in Southern Basketball.

Some of Mississippi's most noted men were born in Smith County near Sullivan's Hollow. Ance McLaurin, before becoming Governor of the State, lived in Smith County. We know him as one of Mississippi's most noble and honest politicians.

The inhabitants of Sullivan's Hollow are red-blooded people as are the inhabitants of any other community. Smith County, which is considered and widely known as the home of Sullivan's Hollow, boasts of its pure Anglo-Saxon blood. No one except this kind of person trods Smith County soil. The population of the county is around 25,000 and of this number there are less than two hundred Negroes. The Negroes of the county are treated with all due respect until such time as he feels his social equality with the white people when he is cast out for the buzzards.[1]

These remarks are racist by nature, but typical of conditions and attitudes of 1930s.

Farming is still essential in Smith County, with soybeans and cattle replacing the small cotton and corn operations. Nice brick farm-

[1]Howell, "Authentic History," 25–27.

houses with expensive machinery of the latest model dot the land-scape.. Electricity is in almost every home. Television antennas are atop each dwelling, and children's rooms come equipped with the latest stereo-decks. Although some of the Sullivan's Hollow roads are still dirt and gravel, they lead to nearby paved roads, which in turn connect to state and federal highways.

Area residents still favor the Ford or Chevrolet over the other models, but an occasional Cadillac or Continental Mark V can be seen in the parking lot of the nearby church. Self-propelled mobile home campers are parked in many garages, and trailer cities have swept over the state like an infestation of grasshoppers. Industry, such as the Georgia Pacific plant, find Smith County a profitable area in which to locate. Young professionals, doctors, teachers, and lawyers are discovering both the financial and personal rewards that come from their labor in rural areas.

Even a romantic idealist would not ask for the inhabitants to go back to the scrubboard and the washtubs on Monday morning or to the "outhouse in the back." No one would want to exchange central heat and air for a drafty house with a fireplace, where in order to be warmed, the women had to back up to the fire holding their skirts up to their loins. Realists would agree that modern schools and school buses are better than trudging miles in the rain or the cold to attend a one-room school heated with a pot-belly stove, and cooled by open-ing the doors and windows to the gnats and flies. No one would deny that the electric blanket is superior to the heated brickbat wrapped in flannel and hastily inserted between the cold sheets, or that a purified system of running cold and hot water is preferable to the old bucket and dipper that served the family and the visitor alike.

A freezer filled with packages of frozen vegetables, fruits, and meat eliminate the necessity of standing over the hot stove hour after hour, twisting the rubber rings and the glass tops onto the Ball glass jars. Moreover, freezing is superior to drying the fruit atop the tin roof of the house! The accessibility of the modern supermarket provides one with a variety of nutritional foods that prevent rickets, pellagra, bloated stomachs, and an early death. Department stores, mail order houses, and a rural free delivery system free the wife from endless hours at the spinning wheel and the foot-pedal sewing machine with its accompanying backache that lasted for more hours than the night afforded sleep.

Tractors, diesels, planters, chemicals, and other agricultural equipment have seen the absolute disappearance of the family mule, the blacksmith, and barnyard manure. Fresh poultry, already dressed and cut-up, has ended the arguments as to whether the Rhode Island Red or Dominecker hen was the best breed of chicken. Working outside the home erased the wife's "egg money" tradition. Children no longer hear of teacake, but know instead the chocolate chip cookie. Ice cream comes in a cone, not out of a churn filled with cooked custard which has simmered on the back of the stove and been turned with eager hands. The after-school snack of a cold tater snatched hastily from the warmer oven of the stove or from the safe in the kitchen has been replaced by the coke and candy bar. The long dress with the bustle in the back and the black, buttoned-up hightop shoes have been usurped by the pantsuit, as has the bowler hat by the fertilizer cap. Children no longer read by the glow of the firelight; in fact they no longer read but watch television instead.

Although slightly altered, many traditions and customs have remained. Despite having dryers in the utility rooms, most housewives still hang their wash out on Mondays. Children still say "yes ma'am" to any woman over twenty. If a man becomes sick or ill, his neighbors will lay by his crop or gather it for him. A disaster, such as a fire, brings a collection of money and clothing for its victim. The crops and the weather remain the chief topics of conversation. The mid-morning question is always, "Has the mail run yet?" Rocking chairs are still the vogue. Many old-timers continue to believe in hot biscuits for breakfast, dressing up for church, and having "cleaning-off-the-cemetery" workdays. Fried chicken and potato salad are a must for Sunday, and the noontime meal is "dinner," not lunch, and the evening meal is still called "supper."

However, there are changes which one regrets. Many young people have left the Hollow to seek employment elsewhere, and many of today's residents are people past thirty-five. Many of the landmark houses have been allowed to fall into disrepair. Abandoned houses are the rule, not the exception. Children no longer look forward to a farm of their own. Many of the farms, cultivated with loving care, which gave to the rolling hills an air of spaciousness have now gone back to scrub oak or have been planted with pines. No longer is the smell of new-cut hay in the air. Few houses now have swept yards, trodden smooth by the bare feet of playing children. No longer do people sit out on the front porch at dusk with their shoes off and their feet propped on the railing. Not many residents use the fireplace with its fragrant aroma of burning oak logs.

Yes, progress has come to the valley; but at what price? Will future generations scoff at the heritage of their forefathers? In their ruthless determination to gratify their own desires, will they lose their sense of community or love of the land? Will the essential vibrant chord of togetherness be lost? Will the same long stretches of congested interstate highways that took the young people to places around the world also be an avenue through which they can return and breathe again the peace and serenity of the old homeplace? Will the old folklore and legends be forever hidden by the day-to-day pressure of carpools, band lessons, and beautyshop appointments until the new generation will be surprised to know they ever existed? Will the lure of jobs awaiting in far-away places cause them to lose forever those ties that have always bound Sullivan to Sullivan? If so, the price was too high; the cost was too dear.

The one important thing that has not changed has been the character of its people: independent, to the point of prideful stubbornness; generous to the poor and wealthy alike; hospitable to the neighbor as well as to the stranger; honest "as the day is long"; proud but not arrogant; a bit rough on exterior but soft on the interior; delightful story-teller. These and many other traits have combined to make these folk a people who will greet you heartily, welcome you among them with a warmth you will never forget, and make those of us who are related to them feel proud that we are from Sullivan's Hollow!

APPENDIX:
The Henderson Sullivan Line

THIS BOOK IS NOT INTENDED as a genealogy of the Sullivan family. Nevertheless, it would not be complete without some genealogical information. Since the story is mainly about the descendants of Henderson Sullivan, his lineage is traced here in detail. This was a mammoth task and the record is by no means complete, since not all family members queried responded, and since census records beyond 1900 are not yet available to the public. However, the genealogy on the Henderson Sullivan line will enable the reader to relate the characters in the book to their position in the family tree.

The following information, moreover, includes a listing of Thomas's other sons and daughters, their spouses, and their children. Information beyond the third generation is not included here. Some inconsistencies appear in census reports, Bible records, cemetery data, and human memories. That such a comprehensive report could be compiled and written about a family so diverse and prolific as the Sullivans is extraordinary.

Henderson's father, Thomas, was born 1785, died 1855, and was married to Maud Elizabeth Arnold (ca. 1790–1846) and to Mary "Polly" Workman (1803–1891). Thomas and both wives are buried in the Hollow in the Alex Sullivan Cemetery. Tom had twenty-two children, twenty of whom had families of their own. His children were:

1.   James "Jim" Sullivan (1810–?) m. Fannie Robertson; his second wife was Patsy Rollins (1826–?). A wooden marker in the Alex Sullivan Cemetery with the inscription "Patsy Sullivan" is located near the grave of her son John Ben. A greatgrandson, James L. Sullivan, president of the Southern Baptist Convention, once remarked that Fannie died of typhoid fever and that Jim went to Mobile, Alabama, to get Patsy whose father was an immigrant from Finland. This information is logical because Thomas's relatives were from north of Mobile, and Jim was probably visiting in that area and became acquainted with the Rollins family. James's children were: Dan B. m. Kate Rutland; Louis (Lewis) m. Emma Grubbs; Wilkie m. Polly Harvey, daughter of Jim's sister, Peggy; John Ben m. Ophelia Evelyn Tuggle; Rufus m. Laura Lee; Edward "Edd" m. Nancy Sullivan,

daughter of Jim's brother, Thomas; Oliver "O. B." m. Margaret Clark; Margaret Jane m. Sam Steele; Clara m. John William Aaron, Sr.,; and Matilda m. John Arthur Cothern.

2. Margaret "Peggy" Sullivan (1812–?) married James "Jake" Harvey, beginning the interrelationship of these two families. Peggy's children were: Mossie m. Warren; Bessie m. Gentry; Isaac "Ike" m. Catherine Gentry; Clara m. Jim Gentry (relationship of these three Gentrys is uncertain); Cassie m. Elias Clark; and Polly m. Wilkie Sullivan, son of James.

3. Thomas Sullivan, Jr. (1814–?), is often referred to as "Hog Tom" because the stories circulated about his reputation for having hogs, many of which he had not raised himself. Since Thomas does not appear in the 1860 census, it can be assumed that he died in the 1850s. His wife, Elizabeth Bishop (1820–?) was listed in 1880 as living with her son, Tillman, but she does not appear in the 1900 schedule. This Bishop family moved to the Hollow shortly after the arrival of Thomas, Sr. The children of Thomas, Jr. were: Willis m. Eliza Bishop Sullivan; Norris m. Maranda "Ran" Rollins (it is not known if she was related to Patsy); Thomas Arnold, sometimes listed as Tom Braddon, m. Ann Patterson, and his second marriage was to Rachael Tew, daughter of Thomas's sister, Clara; William "Billy" m. Mary King; Joseph "Guinea Joe" m. Nancy Butler; Steavie, sometimes listed as never married, although Chester Sullivan records him as having three wives, his last one being Sophronie Ranner; John "Big John" m. Barbara Harvey (perhaps Gentry); Lydia m. Marion Hall; Gracie m. Lidge Ponder; Tillman m. Molly Smith; and Nancy m. Edd "Ed Patsy" Sullivan, son of James and Patsy.

4. Loderick "Lod" Sullivan (1816–1891) m. Elizabeth Tuttle (1822–1907). Both are buried in Good Hope Cemetery near Magee. Children were: Daniel m. Sally Womack; Robinson m. Harriet Sullivan, daughter of Loderick's brother, Henderson; Mary "Polly" m. Tillman Bishop; William M. m. Eliza Garner; Manuel m. Catherine McWilliams; Roderick m. Louisa Fletcher; Willoughby m. Julia Cathern; Garn m. Barzella Woolie; Caroline m. Sam Bowen; Henderson m. Ellen "Tootie" Sullivan, granddaughter of Loderick's brother, Hen-

derson; daughters Elizabeth "Lizzy" and Delila "Dilly" apparently died young.

5. Stephen Sullivan (1816–?) married Mary Dunford. Very little is known about Stephen. His children were: Conn; Thomas "Long Tom" m. Mary Jane Dees; Franklin; Angelina I. m. Thomas Ates; and Steve, who was perhaps the Stephen Sullivan killed at the Battle of Shiloh in the Civil War. Both Stephen, Sr., and Stephen, Jr., served as privates in Co. G, 5th Mississippi Infantry. Stephen, Sr. may also have had two daughters, Amelia and Elizabeth, who died young. Stephen does not appear in any of the census data of Mississippi.

6. Owen Sullivan (1817–?) died young.

7. Joseph Sullivan (1818–1895) married Harriet Wilson (1823–1910), and both are buried at Sardis Church. Their nine children were: Elizabeth m. Bob Wingate; Thomas "Bud" m. Ann Hubbard; Stephen, killed at the Battle of Vicksburg; Orlando Jack m. Ellen K. "Dee" Sullivan, daughter of Joseph's brother, Fredrick; Celia Ann m. Nathan C. West; Joseph, Jr. m. Leah Margaret Sullivan, also a daughter of Fredrick; Mary Margaret m. Thomas Franklin "Money Frank" Sullivan, son of Mark; Wiley A. never married; Sara Jane m. Henderson Sullivan, also a son of Joseph's brother, Mark; Jefferson Davis m. Frances Jane Harvey, granddaughter of Joseph's sister, Peggy, and a daughter of Ike Harvey. Four of these married first cousins. Such intermarriages were typical of Sullivan's Hollow, and were true of many families throughout early American history, especially where the families lived in close proximity and when migration into the locality by outsiders was discouraged.

8. Dan Sullivan (1819–?) died young.

9. Celia Sullivan (1820–?) m. Norris Owen, Sr. (1790–?) and had six children: Sam G. m. Alemeda Knight; Jack m. Beth Knight; Polly "Mary" m. Sam Knight (the relationship between these three Knights was not established); Vashti; Norris, Jr. m. Charity Walker; and Cassandra m. ?

10. Fredrick Sullivan (1821–1897) and his family are fairly well documented, since he left a handwritten record of his children. He married Joanna Louisa (Joanah) Spell (1821–1894), who listed her birthplace as South Carolina. Her brother, John L.,

married Fredrick's younger sister, Mary Ann. In 1850, Fredrick also provided a home for his brother, Jefferson. Both Fredrick and Joanna are buried in the Alex Sullivan Cemetery. Fredrick's oldest daughter was Mary Jane Sullivan who married Francis Marion "Grapps" Howell. Subsequent Sullivans intermarried with the Howell family frequently. Mrs. Sidney (Alma Doris) Howell had done extensive yet unpublished research on the Howell family. Fredrick's other children were: Thomas Jefferson Henderson Sullivan m. Lenora "Pink" Swan; John Wiley "Little Wiley" m. Marion W. Podgett; Louisa Ann Sullivan m. Jasper Ware; Martha Alline "Addie" m. George W. Pickering; Harriet Elizabeth died at four years; Leah Margaret m. Joseph, Jr.; Moranda Catherine "Kate" died at thirteen; George Washington lived only nine years; Ellen Kisiah "Dee" m. Orlando Jack, son of Joseph; and Fredrick Taylor m. Emma Huff.

11. Clara Sullivan (1822–?) m. James "Jim" Tew, who was born in North Carolina. Their oldest son, James A. "Jim" m. Susie "Sis" Rutland; Daniel m. Martha Lee; Sally m. Gabriel "Gabe" Chain (see story in Wild Bill section); Rachael m. Thomas Braddon Sullivan; Nancy m. Henry Hall; and Iverson m. Cynthia Rutland (relationship to Susie unknown).

12. Thomas Jefferson "Jeff" Sullivan (1823–1902) was married three times, first to Mary Stewart, second to Mandy Lucas, and last to Julia Welborn (1856–1921). His firstborn infant died. His other children were: J. J. "Johnny" m. Lucy Wilborn; W. Fred "Lazy Fred" m. Alice Ingram; A. Frank "Walking Frank" m. Polly Ann Grace; George M. m. Mattie Grace; Harvey never married but lived to be forty-nine years old; Polie m. Annie Wells; Hardy never married; and Dallas m. Minnie Stewart. There is conflicting evidence as to the date of Jeff's death, which is listed as 1893, 1897, and 1902 in various places. He is buried in the Alex Cemetery.

13. Caroline Sullivan (1824–1872) m. H. Allen Byrd (1801–?). Their eldest son, James Allen Byrd, m. Sarah Elizabeth Howell, daughter of William Howell, the founder of the Howell family in Smith County; Thomas R. "Raz" had three wives—Louisa Fill, Kate Stokes, and Mary E. Wilkins; Paul M. m. Henrietta S.

"Duck" or "Shuck" Ware; the only daughter, Ellen E. Byrd m. John Wesley Gentry. Allen and Caroline are buried in the Byrd Cemetery, west of Mize.

14. Henderson "Hense" Sullivan lineage is traced separately in the latter part of this chapter.

15. Eliza Jane Sullivan (1827–1890) m. Calvin Ates (b. ca. 1822) and they had ten children; two (Janey and Catherine Eliza) died in infancy. The other children were: Mary Ann m. Bryant Kirkland; John Wiley m. Juriah Sellars; Frances Adeline m. Samuel Willbanks; Samuel Harper m. Charity Lucas; William Brewer m. Laura Willbanks; Calvin Newton m. Matilda E. Lott; Loten Celvanus m. Josephina Lawrence; and Harmon Van Buren m. Octavia Peoples. Eliza and Calvin Ates are buried in Willbanks Cemetery, East Feliciana Parish, Ball, Louisiana.

16. Mark Sullivan (1830–1913) served in the 8th Infantry, C.S.A., was courtmartialed for being AWOL, but was saved by his captain, George Buchanan. He and his wife Catherine "Cathy" Byrd (1832–1872) had seven children, although she died at the age of forty. Their children were: Celia Jane m. George B. Ashley; Thomas Franklin "Money Frank" m. Mary Margaret Sullivan; Robert Henderson m. Sarah Jane Sullivan; Laura C., who died in 1875 at the age of thirteen; Mark A. "Mack" m. Virginia Estella "Stella" Sullivan; Mary Margaret m. Hiram Sellars; and Tabithia Sullivan m. Pete Robinson. Three of Mark's grandchildren married sons or daughters of Judge William Marion Howell. Mark and Cathy are buried in the Alex Sullivan Cemetery in Sullivan's Hollow.

17. Wiley P. "Big Wiley" Sullivan (1832–1904) married Annie Terrissa (Ann) Reddock (1832–1893). They had eleven children: Ezekial Q. "Zeke" m. Margaret Harvey; William Wiley m. Florence Harvey; Eliza m. Willey (Willie) Flint; Mary Ellen m. Taylor Smith; Elvin J., who died young; Samuel A. m. Ella Woodward; Laura C. m. Ed W. Norris; Martha Mahala m. Nicholas Ben Craft; Altimara "Alice" m. Andrew Jack (son of Wild Bill) and after his death, she married Lewis Luck; Ollie m. George "Hank" Allen; and Claudia m. Brown Luke Norris. Since two of Big Wiley's sons married Harveys and two daughters married a Norris, there were close ties between

these two families. At Bunker Hill, Wiley Sullivan and Marion Howell put up one of the first water-powered sawmills in Smith County. Big Wiley and his wife are buried in Alex Sullivan Cemetery.

18.   Mary Ann Sullivan (1835–1924) m. John L. Spell (1832–1913). John was a brother of Joanna, who married Mary's brother Fredrick Sullivan. John and Mary Ann's children were: Charity Ellen m. William Dave Darden; William Luther "Willie" m. Mary Elizabeth Sullivan, daughter of Cornelius; John Alexander (known as "Alex" in the story of Wild Bill's trial), who never married; Samuel Loten m. Fannie Elizabeth Dickerson; Joanna Eliza m. Willie Harvey; and Alexandria, who apparently never married. The Spells are buried in Zion Hill Cemetery.

19.   Samuel R. Sullivan (middle name unknown) (1838–1917). Private, Company C, 8th Infantry, C.S.A., married Sarah E. Hathorne (1843–1924). Their children were: Ora Anna m. Frank Ashley; Mary Kessiah (never married) was known as "Kizzie"; Robert Edward, for whom the Ed Sullivan Cemetery is named, m. Mary Jane, daughter of Wild Bill; K. Oliver (K. O.) m. Joanna Tilson; W. Alonzo m. Ella Keyes; Beulah Lee was the second wife of Francis Marion Howell, and her second husband was Albert Smith; Abel Eugene m. Annie Lulla Sullivan; and Nevada "Vada" m. Cleve Sullivan, with Mark Ashley being her second husband. Another child died in infancy. Samuel R. is buried in Alex Sullivan Cemetery, while Sarah is interred in Old Zion Cemetery near Mt. Olive.

20.   Cornelius J. "Conn" Sullivan (1838–1917) is the son who lived in the log house with his mother, Mary Workman, after Thomas died. The years of his birth and death are variously recorded. Conn married Jane Wigginton (or Willington?) (1848–1882) and after her death, he married Betty Hightower (1850–?). Conn was listed in ninth (1870) census as a school teacher, but subsequent schedules list him as a farmer. Conn's children were: George m. Inda Woodward; Mary m. Willie Spell; Luther B. m. Birdie Spell; Margaret Ellen, unmarried; Ezra m. Lydia Sullivan; Eliza m. Green Harvey; and Joanna m. Jake Warren. The parents are buried in Zion Hill Cemetery.

21. Loughton "Loten" Sullivan (1844–1898) m. Martha Jo "Matt" West (1850–1907). They later left the Hollow (see story of Wild Bill) and are buried near Bassfield, Mississippi. Their fourteen children were: Thomas Wilson m. Sara Jane Howell, daughter of S. M. Howell; Sardis Mark m. Mag Keyes; Mary Leona "Molly" m. J. T. Mayfield; Martha Lela m. Joe C. Walker; Emma Zora m. Isaac Keyes; Ira m. Sally Pope; Otha m. Maybelle McDonald; Ettie m. Laurin Magee; Blanch Ellen m. William Jacob Carter; Irma Eliza m. Joe McDonald; Beulah Jo m. Carley Robertson; O. Ulysses m. Jennie Lewis; N. D. died at seven years of age; and Cuma E. m. J. W. Stewart. Sons Ira and Otha were ministers.

22. Alexander Sullivan (1847–1937) m. Maryan Catherine Keyes (1848–1922). This youngest son of Thomas and Mary Workman is the one for whom the Alex Sullivan Cemetery is named. Their eleven children were: Robert T. "Bob" m. Molly Wingate; Benjamin A. m. Annie M. Russell; William J., died in infancy; Lula m. Tom Flynt; Alice Elizabeth m. Joseph Keyes; E. Fred m. Fannie C. Sullivan; Ester Ellen m. Volney Keyes (who lived in the log house at one time); Ester's twin sister, Hester M., lived less than a month; Anna m. Robert M. Russell who also lived in the log house and probably added the second pen, remodeling the house extensively; Quincy A. m. Mattie L. Sullivan as his first wife and Fannie Rassum as his second wife; and Rassie C. m. Bertha Harvey.

Since descendants from Thomas can now be traced to the ninth generation, it is difficult to estimate the number of persons in Mississippi who have his blood coursing in their veins. Many of his descendants live in other states. Moreover, to write the complete genealogy of all the related families would require a lifetime of research.

This section also enumerates the descendants of Henderson "Hense" Sullivan, the fourteenth child of Thomas. Henderson's lineage is traced here in detail since he was the father of Wild Bill. Henderson's mother was Mary Workman. His exact birthdate is not known. On his tombstone the date is 1814, but Dovie Sullivan reports the date to be conjectural and guessed at by her Aunt Zona.

Since the 1850 census lists him as being twenty-five years old and the 1880 census as fifty-four, he was born in either 1825 or 1826; however, from the 1870 census his birthdate could be 1830. In Maxine Watt's records his birthdate is August 21, 1825. Henderson died in 1898 and is buried in the Ed Sullivan Cemetery.

Hense's wife, Leah Howell, consistently gave her age. Thus her birthdate is 1827 or 1828, depending upon which month of the year the census taker gathered the information. Again, Aunt Zona guessed at her birth as being 1816. Her name is spelled incorrectly on her headstone as "Leria." In the tenth (1880) census, she was listed as "L. J." but in others simply as Leah. Her parents were William Howell and Elizabeth McLemore. William was the founder of the Sullivan's Hollow Howells, and apparently migrated to the Hollow from Kentucky. His marriage to Betsy was listed in Lawrence County, Mississippi, records as February 20, 1827. Leah was the sister of Francis Marion Howell, who married Henderson's niece, Mary Jane Sullivan. Another of Leah's sisters, Sarah Elizabeth Howell, married Jim A. Byrd, Thomas's grandson in that line of the family. Numerous other intermarriages of the Howell-Sullivan families occurred in later generations.

For simplification, Henderson is listed here as 14.0; his ten children will be listed as 14.1 to 14.10 with their children coded as 14.1.1, etc. A designation such as "14.1.3.4.6" means that that person is the sixth child of the fifth generation, and is descended from the fourth child of the third child of the first child of Henderson. Furthermore, all descendants on whom information is available will be listed for each of Henderson's children before another child's family is reported. In this way, a person's direct lineage can be determined.

The Henderson
Sullivan Line

14.0 Henderson Sullivan m. Leah Howell

14.1 Cornelius "Neece" Sullivan (1845–1920)
    m. 1. Emily O. Gibbeons Howell
    m. 2. _____ White
    m. 3. Alabama Earla (Allie) Milner
14.1.1. George N. Sullivan m. Maggie Burkhalter
    1. Meddie C. m. Dora Holifield
    2. Nora m. _____ Parker
    3. Lena m. John Gandy
    4. Trudy m. _____ Rogers
14.1.2. Stephen Henderson "Hense" Sullivan m. Ophelia Burkhalter
    1. Alberta "Bertie" or "Birdie" m. Wiley Wood
        1. Lutie Emily Wood m. Jimmy Switzer
        2. Lottis Ray Wood m. Curtis Switzer
        3. Hense Wood m. Lillian Logan
        4. Dent Wood m. Belle Brown
        5. John Mack Wood m. Joan Grissom
        6. Billy Wood m. Frances Lewis
        7. Jerry Kenneth Wood
        8. Paul Wood m. Waudine Byrd
        9. Ophelia Wood m. Billy Harper
    2. Dovie "Della" Sullivan m. Clarence Horn
        1. Jess Edith Horn m. Chalmer Corley
        2. Whitfield Horn
        3. Clarence Horn
        4. Ethel Horn m. Pat Leggett
    3. Lamar Sullivan m. Ethel Wilson
        1. Chester Sullivan
        2. Carrie Sullivan
    4. Ethel Sullivan (died young)

     5. Flossie Darleen Sullivan m. Walter Marion King
     6. Mattie D. Sullivan m. John Elton "Rassie" Gunter
       1. Hilda Gunter
       2. Charles Gunter
       3. Sally Gunter
       4. Doris Gunter
       5. John D. Gunter
       6. Dimple Gunter
       7. Jimmy F. Gunter
       8. Sandra Gunter
     7. Lavell Sullivan m. Margie Hawkins
       1. J. L. Sullivan
       2. Lodessa Sullivan m. Kenneth Cox
         1. Michael Cox
         2. Susan Cox
         3. Randal Cox
       3. Jane Sullivan m. Leroy Yates
       4. Dennis Sullivan
       5. Carolyn Sullivan
       6. Richard Sullivan
     8. Stone Devoures Sullivan m. Margie Sullivan
       1. Joan E. Sullivan m. Walter Skipper
       2. Jeannette Ophelia Sullivan m. Charles Cole
         1. Michelle Leigh Cole
       3. Rebecca Ann Sullivan m. Billy H. Wallace
         1. Christy Lane Wallace
       4. Brenda Jo Sullivan m. Charles Adcock
         1. Jennifer Deneice Adcock
       5. Michael Cornelius Sullivan
     9. Inez Sullivan m. Orange Glendon Gunter
       1. Mary Lou Gunter
14.1.3. Robert Joshua "Josh" Sullivan
    m. 1. Nancy Bonita Hall
    m. 2. Mary Harvey Temple
    1. Travis Cornelius Sullivan m. Ethel Jones
       1. Frances Sullivan m. Lester Burnham
       2. Avis Sullivan m. Edsel Gibbons
       3. Cornelia (never married)
    2. Alma Rose Sullivan m. Ledrow Bane Mathis
       1. Helen Mathis m. Desmond Craft
       2. Jacqueline Mathis m. Jake Shivers
       3. Aurelia Mathis m. Jimmy Quinn
       4. Charlotte Amy Mathis
    3. Stephen Hooper Sullivan m. Tiny Sullivan
       1. Tiny Sullivan

4. George Thomas Sullivan m. Estelle Walters
   1. Syble Sullivan m. ?
   2. George Thomas m. Sadie Riley
5. William Earle Sullivan m. Thelma Harvey
   1. Bennet Sullivan m. Dorothy Giles
      1. William Mark Sullivan
   2. Sennet Sullivan m. Pearl Brumfield
      1. Royce Earl Sullivan
      2. Nancy Carol Sullivan m. Doyle Ross
6. Minnie Altie Sullivan m. Everett Burnham
   1. Robert Lewis Burnham m. Mary Roy King
7. Ruth Leona m. Delton West
   1. Hubert West
   2. Hulon West
   3. Danny West
8. Ruby Sullivan m. Walter V. Roberson
   1. W. J. Roberson
   2. Johnie Merle Roberson
9. Allie Sullivan (died young)
10. Pearlie Orine Sullivan m. Edgar Robertson
11. Merle Sullivan m. Forest Smith
   1. Bonita Ann m. John Larry Sullivan
12. Jeffie Ree Sullivan m. Colbert Sharp
   1. Robert Maxwell Sharp
   2. Brenda Sue Sharp
   3. Anthony Sharp
   4. Deborah Ann Sharp

14.1.4. C. Frank "Bud Neese" Sullivan m. Ida Mae Wood
1. Bessie J. Sullivan m. Clifton Sullivan
   1. Flora Sullivan m. Fred Hands
2. R. C. Sullivan
3. Craven Sullivan m. Mae Sullivan
   1. Henry E. Sullivan m. Nelda Davis
   2. Annie Sullivan m. Billy Zeigler
   3. Newell Sullivan m. Vondell Bryant
   4. Roscoe Sullivan m. Betty Young
      1. William David Sullivan
      2. Sherrie Lynn Sullivan
   5. Mary Jo Sullivan m. Truett Weatherford
      1. Mary Diane Weatherford
   6. Billy Wayne Sullivan
4. John L. Sullivan
5. Bob Sullivan
6. Horace Sullivan
7. Billie Sullivan

14.1.5. Kate C. Sullivan m. Benjamin F. "Ben" Harvey
    1. Idelle Harvey
    2. Lowen Harvey m. Mary Jane Sellers
       1. Franklin Harvey
    3. Archie Harvey m. Myrtis Crews
    4. Ana Harvey m. Jim Crews
    5. Nezzie Harvey m. Homer Harvey
       1. Patricia Harvey
    6. Verdie Harvey
14.1.6. Beatrice A. Sullivan m. Isaac F. "Bud" Harvey
    1. Bertha Harvey m. Rassie C. Sullivan
       1. Etoyle Sullivan
          m. 1. Thomas W. Sullivan
          m. 2. Nevil Cranford Sullivan
             1. Ray Gerald Sullivan m. Janice Wade
                1. Ray Gerald Sullivan
                2. Allen Sullivan
             2. Patricia Sullivan m. Rayburn "Punk" Lancaster
                1. Leslie Caren Lancaster
                2. Jason Lancaster
    2. Mamie Harvey m. Chester Sullivan, son of "Puss"
    3. Minnie Harvey m. Oliver Stewart
    4. Varnie Harvey m. Rob Sullivan, grandson of Alex
    5. Lavelle Harvey m. Thelma Stringer
14.1.7. Effie Sullivan
    m. 1. Louis Lucky
    m. 2. B. Madden Sullivan
    m. 3. Wharton H. "Will" Woolwine
       1. Luldrus Lucky
       2. Luther Lucky
       3. Artie Sullivan m. John Harwell
       4. Carl Sullivan
       5. Ethel C. Sullivan m. Hazel Carter
       6. Cecil Woolwine
       7. Clayton Woolwine
       8. _____ Woolwine m. C. B. Whiddon
14.1.8. Mac Sullivan m. Lora Pardue
    1. Robert Neace Sullivan m. Mary Joyce Windham
       1. Joyce Ann Sullivan
       2. Stephanie Roberts Sullivan
       3. Robin Elise Sullivan
       4. Robert Nease Sullivan (died infant)
       5. Robert Mack Sullivan
       6. Michael Adams Sullivan

7. Willie Carl Sullivan

14.2. Mary Sullivan (b. 1847) m. Quit Reddock
(No further information on this family)

14.3 Anna Sullivan (b. 1850) m. W. R. "Bob" Gibbons
14.3.1. Louisa Gibbons m. J. S. Bishop
    1. Martin Bishop
    2. Lucille Bishop
    3. Harris Cornelius Bishop
14.3.2. Nancy J. Gibbons
14.3.3. Rufus Gibbons
14.3.5. Harriet Gibbons
14.3.6. William Gibbons

14.4. William Cicero "Wild Bill" Sullivan m. Juriah Keyes
14.4.1. Julius Evander Sullivan
    m. 1. Sarah Elizabeth Ates
    m. 2. Mary Etta Wallace
    1. Nancy Carolyn "Carrie" Sullivan m. Robert Craven Howell
        1. Robert Gavin Howell m. Velma Adams Gibson
            1. Burnis Milton Howell m. Mary Ruth Fisher
                1. Rickey Milton Howell
                2. Sharon Ruth Howell
            2. Jessie Craven Howell m. Margarette Hobby
                1. Nancy Rebecca Howell
                2. Margaretta Michelle Howell
                3. Audria Howell
                4. Erma Lenae Howell
            3. Carlton Edwin Howell m. Sue Whitaker
                1. Wanda Sue Howell
                2. Shelia Ann Howell
                3. Diane Charlotte Howell
        Robert Gavin Howell
        m. 2. Lillie Belle Rivers
            No children
        m. 3. Ester Havard Reeves
            No children
    2. Walter Milton "Pat" Howell m. Eunice Juanita Dake
        1. Carolyn Juanita Howell m. Billy Ray Harrison
            1. Sean Allen Harrison
            2. Shannon Leanne Harrison
            3. Shane Ray Harrison
        2. Darryl Milton Howell m. Nancy Fretz
            1. Judy Michele Howell

     3. Eula Mae Frances Howell m. Eldon Obtine Robertson
       1. Infant son died
     4. Myrn'l Elizabeth "Monk" Howell m. Vaden Dubose
       1. Kenneth Vaden Dubose m. Sandra Canfield
         1. Kenneth Wayne Dubose
         2. Melinda Joelen Dubose
         3. Charlotte Michele Dubose
       2. Thomas Merle Dubose m. Linda Carolyn Williams
         1. Bobbie Carol Dubose
         2. Teresa Dennise Dubose
         3. Billy James Dubose
       3. Myrna Ann Dubose
     5. Jessie Bobbie Nell Howell m. Joseph Simeon Collier
       1. Robert Wayne Collier m. Barbara Ann Lopey
         1. Sonja Marie Collier
         2. Robert DeWayne Collier
         3. Monique Collier
     6. Carolyn Lalarook Howell m. Gilbert Steele Mitchell
       1. Janice Lea Mitchell
       2. Chester Allen Mitchell
       3. Anita Carol Mitchell
14.4.1.2. Milton Clarence Sullivan
    m. 1. Lula Virginia Maddox
       1. Clarence Milton "Demp" Sullivan m. Edna Ramsey
         1. Cynthai Ann Sullivan m. Sidney Hudson
    m. 2. Nellie Jewel Marble
       2. Mary Elizabeth Sullivan
         m. 1. John Henry Forbes
         m. 2. Warren D. Fortenberry
    m. 3. Bessie Bernice Marble
       3. John Lewis Sullivan (unmarried)
14.4.1.3. Eula Sullivan m. Virgil Marion Howell
     1. Randolph Pruitt Howell (died young)
     2. Hilda Howell (unmarried)
     3. Fannie Mae Howell m. John Norman Smith
       1. Patricia Kaye Smith (died)
       2. Wanda Rae Smith m. Earl Stephens
         1. Norman Shannon Stephens
     3. Annie Ray Howell m. Ray Otto Hammons
       1. Mary Ann Hammons m. Fredrick Eugene Harmon, Jr.
         1. Sandra Gayle Harmon
         2. Patricia Susan Harmon
         3. Cathryn Meredith Harmon
       2. Lynda Frances Hammons m. Gorman Clayte Eidson, Jr.
         1. Pamela Lynn Eidson
         2. Debra Ann Eidson

3. Michael Clayte Eidson
3. Beverly Sue Hammons m. James Darrell Bryner
    4. Ray Otto Hammons, Jr. (died)
5. Virginia Myrnal Howell m. (1) Macel Lafayette
                     Canterbury
                    (2) Lloyd Anderson
  1. Judy Amanda Canterbury
  2. Macel Lafayette Canterbury, Jr. m. Christine Dotson
    1. Dewayne Canterbury
    2. David Canterbury
    3. M. L. Canterbury, III
    4. Crystal Lee Canterbury
  3. Billie Howell Canterbury m. Bobby Jean Cook
    1. Delanya Diane Canterbury
    2. Billie Howell Canterbury, Jr.
  4. Paul Dwight Canterbury
  5. Frances Abelene Canterbury m. William Kemp
  6. Virgil Wayne Canterbury m. Stella Wheeler Bierbaum
6. Marion Lehonne Howell m. Gladys Louise Barnes
  1. William Marion "Skipper" Howell
    m. 1. Carolyn Ann Young
    m. 2. Patricia Hare
    1. Dawn Marie Howell
    2. Jeffrey Lee Howell
  2. Kinnon Hunter Howell
    m. 1. Dorothy June Lange
    m. 2. Kathleen Ruble
    1. Kinnon Hunter Howell, Jr.
  3. Debra Louise Howell m. James C. Seymour, Jr.
  4. Mark Lowell Howell (died in infancy)
7. Leroy Hunter "Jack" Howell m. Mary Louise Netterville
  1. Leroy Hunter Howell, Jr.
  2. Charles Virgil Howell m. Elizabeth Lynn Culp
    1. Charles Dustin Howell
  3. Marilyn Eloise Howell
  4. Rachael Melinda Howell
8. Dixie Carlos Howell m. Lois Bernell Adkins
  1. William Marion Adkins
  2. Robert Samuel Adkins
  3. Nell Adkins
  4. Ann Howell Adkins
14.4.1.4. Harvey Melvin Sullivan (died young)
14.4.1.5. Vernie Sullivan (died young)
14.4.1.6. Shelford "Shep" Bush Sullivan m. Dovie Jane Howell
  1. Mary Beryl Sullivan (died young)

    2. Geraldine "Boots" Sullivan m. Bidwell A. Owens
       1. Naomi Jane Owens m. Merlyn Ray Dungey
          1. Adam Dungey
          2. Wendy Dungey
          3. Erin Dungey
       2. Gerry Owens m. Marty Hull
       3. Bidwell A. Owens, Jr. m. Margaret Pittman
       4. Robert Shelford Owens
    3. Paul Arthur Sullivan m. Theresa Lamanca
       1. Kim Sullivan m. Deborah Garner
       2. Yvonne Sullivan
       3. Michael Paul Sullivan
       4. Gregory Dean Sullivan
    4. Janith Ann Sullivan m. Shelton Gerald Allen
       1. Jerri Leigh Allen
       2. Karen Allen
       3. Marty Pierre Allen
    5. Vernie Marion Sullivan m. Margaret Elizabeth Dyess
       1. Kelli Michelle Sullivan
       2. Jeffrey Scott Sullivan
14.4.1.7. Charlie Lewis Sullivan m. Lora Holdcroft
    1. Norma Sullivan m. Bobby Bruner
       1. Michael Bruner
    2. Joyce Sullivan m. George Smith
       1. Becky Smith
       2. Chris Smith
       3. Marty Smith
       4. Allen Smith
    3. Charles Linden Sullivan m. Helen Byrd
       1. Charles Linden Sullivan, Jr.
       2. Lewis Ervin Sullivan
       3. Denise Sullivan
       4. Liza Sullivan
       5. Melanie Sullivan
       6. Timothy Sullivan
       7. Johnny Sullivan
       8. Kim Sullivan
    4. Daniel Sullivan m. Verna Ledford
       1. Daniel Sullivan
       2. Charlotte Sullivan
       3. Duane Sullivan
    5. Terry Sullivan m. Vadette Wilburn
       1. Johnny Sullivan
       2. Holly Sullivan
       3. Chris Sullivan
       4. Kipp Sullivan

      6. Larry Sullivan m. Arin Phillips
        1. Carla Sullivan
        2. Lavon Sullivan
      7. Laverne Sullivan
14.4.1. Julius Sullivan
      m. 2. Mary Etta Wallace
14.4.1.8. Merle Sullivan m. William J. Walters
      1. Johnny Roberts Walters
      2. Brenda Cheryl Walters m. Dennis McDonald
14.4.1.9. Bradis Sullivan m. L. J. Dickerson
      1. Ann Dickerson m. Oden Banks Tanner
        1. Bridgett Tanner
14.4.1.10. Maybelle Sullivan m. Kenneth Lacy
      1. Judy Lacy
      2. Buddy Lacy
      3. Linda Lacy
      4. Kathy Lacy
      5. Vicky Lacy
14.4.1.11. Nevil Cranford Sullivan m. Etoyle Sullivan
14.4.1.12. Dorothy Sullivan m. Eddie Eggerson
      1. Huey Eggerson
      2. Sharon Eggerson
      3. Chris Eggerson
14.4.1.13. Herbert Sullivan (unmarried)
14.4.2. Mary Jane Sullivan m. Robert Edward Sullivan
      1. Infant son
      2. Minnie Sullivan m. Lee Martin
        1. Adrain Martin
        2. Gerald Martin
      3. Hines J. Sullivan
        m. 1. Maggie Mae Ford
        m. 2. Winnie Duff King
        1. James Edward Sullivan m. Wilse Welbourne
        2. Ralph Sullivan m. Geraldine Ford
        3. Tammie Sullivan m. Dennis McGraw
      4. Cuba Sullivan m. Lattis Jones
        1. Paul Jones
        2. Edward Jones
      5. Bob Sullivan m. Gilmer Godbold
        1. Edward Sullivan
        2. Jane Sullivan
        3. Harry Sullivan
        4. Pat Sullivan
      6. Ulma Sullivan m. Joel Thomas Puckett
        1. Odean Puckett
        2. Viola Puckett

7. Gilbert Sullivan m. Sallie Ruth Freeny
   1. Herbert Sullivan
   2. Ann Sullivan
   3. Jerry Sullivan
14.4.3. Andrew Jackson "Jack" Sullivan m. Altimara "Alice" Sullivan
   1. Volus P. Sullivan m. Della Margaret Spell
      1. Janette Sullivan m. L. B. "Punchie" Tillson
   2. Eunice Sullivan m. J. P. Sullivan
      1. Jerry Sullivan m. Audrey McLaurin
      2. Jessie Ruth Sullivan m. Junior Luke
      3. Peggy Nell Sullivan m. Earl Hodge
      4. Annette Sullivan m. Thomas F. Sullivan
   3. Bonnie J. Sullivan m. William Sylvester Spell
      1. Dorie Spell m. Gatha Creel
      2. Mary Alice Spell m. Hollis Hodge
      3. Sylvia Ann Spell m. Sydney Neil
      4. Delma Spell m. Earl Wells
      5. Ned Spell m. Jimmie Phillips
      6. Jack Spell m. Gladys Dredsby
      7. Gerald Spell m. Marie _____ (a German)
      8. William Earl Spell m. Charlene Maddox
      9. W. B. Spell m. Winnie Johnston
     10. Thomas Spell m. Linda Griffith
     11. Charles Spell m. Ava _____
   4. Andrew Jack Sullivan, Jr.
     m. 1. Myrtle Howell
     m. 2. Hattie Wade
      1. Vernon Dee Sullivan m. Boneda McLauren
      2. Andrew Jack Sullivan III m. Bettie Jo King
      3. Hilda Marie "Judy" Sullivan m. James Burley Howell
      4. Bobbie Joe Sullivan m. Irene Larosa
   5. Emma Sullivan m. Robert Dupree
      1. L. L. Dupree m. Pearl Johnson
         1. Bobby Jean Dupree
         2. Thomas Leroy Dupree
         3. Linda Ann Dupree
         4. Dorothy Louise Dupree
         5. Joy Lanell Dupree
      2. Louise Dupree m. Clyde Corbin
         1. Oliver Gerald Corbin
         2. David Ray Corbin
         3. Harry Earl Corbin
         3. Larry Merl Corbin
         5. Tussie Louise Corbin
      3. Willie Ray Dupree m. Hattie Mae Corbin
         1. Diana Dupree

2. Gloria Jean Dupree
3. Jessie Ruth Dupree
4. Vicky Susan Dupree
4. Tommy Joe Dupree m. Bobbie Lou Snooks
    1. Brenda Joe Dupree
    2. Douglas Wayne Dupree
    3. Jeanette Dupree
5. Jimmie Dale Dupree m. Norma Whitten
    1. Jewel Dene Dupree
    2. Jimmie Dale Dupree, Jr.
6. Evelyn Joyce Dupree m. Bill Beauregard
7. Irene Dupree m. James L. Waynewright
8. Ann "Tootsie" Dupree
9. Wayne Dupree

14.4.4. Martha Ann "Molly" Sullivan m. Thomas Elbert Pickering
1. George Dewey Pickering m. Lena Sullivan
2. Elbert Pickering (unmarried)
3. Sylvester Pickering m. Cleora Sullivan
    1. Clinton Pickering m. Helen Joel
        1. Glenda Faye Pickering
    2. Randel Pickering m. Myrtle Thrum
        1. Randy Lynn Pickering
        2. Bobby Pickering
        3. Debra Pickering
    3. Herbert Pickering (unmarried)
    4. Hershel Pickering m. Carmon Kemp
        1. James Pickering
        2. Marsha Pickering
        3. Mitchell Pickering
        4. Kenneth Pickering
    5. Mary Ann Pickering m. Huey Chellette
        1. Brenda Gail Chellette
        2. Robin Wayne Chellette
        3. Janice Chellette
        4. Carl David Chellette
    6. Rudolph Pickering m. Mary A. Revardia
        1. Darlene Pickering
        2. Patricia Pickering
        3. Marvin Pickering
        4. Marty Pickering
    7. Adrian Pickering m. Emily Revardia
        1. James Pickering
        2. Tina Marie Pickering
    8. Doris Mae Pickering
        m. 1. James Neely
        m. 2. Joe Gautney

        9. Gerald Pickering m. Carolyn _____
          1. Kimberly Ann Pickering
          2. Mark Herman Pickering
    4. Infant son, died
    5. Mattie Pickering m. Newman Craft
    6. Lena Pickering m. Dan Howell
    7. Chester Pickering m. Ardell Morris
        1. Barbara Helen Pickering m. James Bailey
          1. Dorothy Ann Bailey
          2. James Bailey
        2. Hazel Pickering m. Claude Henderson
          1. Marsha Henderson
          2. Howard Henderson
          3. Joel Henderson
        3. Robert Thomas Pickering m. Elaine Alderman
          1. Janet Dianne Pickering
          2. Melody Ann Pickering
        4. Chester Pickering
        5. James Roy Pickering m. Katherine Ezell
          1. Connie Jean Pickering
    8. Lee Pickering m. Ola Pauline Runnells
    9. Rosa Pickering m. Clifton Wade
   10. Rachel Pickering m. Oscar Rawls
   11. John Mack Pickering m. Edna Self
14.4.5. Bobbie Sullivan (killed, age 20)
14.4.6. Arizona "Zona" Sullivan m. Wiley Joseph "Smoking Joe" Sullivan
    1. Minnie Ury Sullivan (died young)
    2. John Sharp Sullivan (died young)
    3. Cammie Louella Sullivan (died young)
    4. Wiley Joseph Adams Sullivan m. Mary Esther Richards
        1. Bill Banker Sullivan
    5. Pershing Boyd Sullivan m. Pauline Brewer
        1. Pershing Boyd Sullivan, Jr.
        2. Jane Sullivan
        3. Mike Sullivan
14.4.7. Myrtle Sullivan m. Herman S. Bryant
    1. Dicey Bryant m. Carl Yelverton
        1. Cleta Yelverton m. Doug Mager
        2. Dale Yelverton m. Doug Baldwin
        3. Lawanda Yelverton
    2. Hazel Bryant m. Dr. Carthell Welbourn
14.4.8. George Boyd Sullivan
    m. 1. Mary Hall
    m. 2. Joyce _____

m. 3. Bradis Ainsworth
   1. Bettie Sullivan

14.5. Louisa Jane Sullivan
14.5.1. W. Taylor Sullivan m. Della Wood
14.5.2. Narvel R. "Dick" Sullivan m. Elizabeth "Bettie" Sullivan
14.5.3. Effie J. Sullivan (unmarried)
14.5.4. Chester Sullivan m. Mamie Harvey
   1. Estelle Sullivan m. Walter Lewis Richardson
   2. Ray Sullivan
   3. Willie B. Sullivan m. Tom Powell
14.5.5. Sarah Ann Sullivan m. Walter Dickerson
   1. Vera Dickerson (unmarried)
   2. Glen Dickerson m. _____ Craft
   3. Elnora Dickerson m. J. W. Sullivan
14.5.6. Ellen "Toodie" Sullivan m. Henderson Sullivan
   1. Willoughby Sullivan m. _____
   2. Kiley Sullivan m. _____
   3. Clemie Sullivan m. Glaston Sullivan
   4. Lillian Sullivan m. Leonard Sullivan
   5. _____ m. Ed Wells
   6. _____ m. Alonzo Wells

14.6. Henderson "Henry" Sullivan, Jr. m. Mary Eubanks
14.6.1. Jesse Myer Sullivan m. Ida Jane Sullivan
   1. Gatha Sullivan m. _____ Rogers
   2. Glaston Sullivan m. Clemmie Sullivan
   3. Helen Sullivan m. Albert Rogers
   4. Vernell Sullivan m. R. C. King
14.6.2. James Monroe Sullivan m. Myrtle J. Axton
   1. Clinton Sullivan m. Elbamae Runnels
   2. Barney Sullivan m. Evelyn Stroud
   3. James Sullivan m. Helen Mangum
14.6.3. Levi Sullivan (unmarried ?)
14.6.3. Leon Sullivan m. Beulah Blakeney
   1. Elwin Sullivan m. Ulma Rae Rutland
   2. Bedelle Sullivan m. _____
14.6.5. Clarence Sullivan m. Sarah Ann Darden
   1. Ulma Sullivan m. Ronald Powell
   2. Hazel Sullivan m. Archie Coffield
   3. L. D. Sullivan (unmarried)
   4. Clarence, Jr. m. Pearline Jones
14.6.6. Robert Lowery Sullivan m. Bettie Ware
   1. Ennis S. Sullivan m. Ruby Moore
   2. Era Sullivan m. Rufus Harrison

      3. Henry D. Sullivan m. Christine Major
      4. Mary Loy Sullivan m. R. W. Ashley
      5. Maggie Sue Sullivan m. Curtis Bryant
      6. Roland Dale Sullivan m. Billie Mae Boykin
14.6.7. Henderson Sullivan, Jr. m. Minnie Ashley
      1. Jewel Sullivan m. Candice McDaniel
      2. Etha Sullivan m. Harlan Byan
      3. Alice Rae Sullivan m. Herbert McCollum
      4. Myrtis Sullivan m. Gary White
      5. Norvil Sullivan m. Bradis Yelverton
      6. Hollis Sullivan m. Wilma Martin
      7. Ruby Gay Sullivan m. Billie Westmoreland
14.6.8. Ellis Sullivan m. Susie Robinson
14.6.9. Nola Sullivan m. William McLaurin
      (Spouses of children not known)
      1. L. B. McLaurin
      2. Bessie McLaurin
      3. Willie Joy McLaurin
      4. Nelma McLaurin
      5. Janette McLaurin
      6. Linton McLaurin
      7. Bobbie McLaurin
      8. Audrey McLaurin
      9. Oneida McLaurin
14.6.10. Elizabeth "Betty" Sullivan m. Narvel R. Sullivan

14.7 Andrew Jack "Red Jack" Sullivan m. Laura Meadows
14.7.1. Sally Sullivan m. Sid Chambers
14.7.2. Alfred Sullivan m. Annie Ophelia Allen
14.7.3. Bella Sullivan m. George Wade
14.7.4. J. P. Sullivan m. Eunice Sullivan
      (children listed at 14.4.3.2)
14.7.5. Molly Sullivan
      m. 1. Will Alexander
      m. 2. Fed White
14.7.6. Estella Sullivan m. Ed Millings
14.7.7. Lona Sullivan m. Archie McDaniel

14.8 Harriet Sullivan m. Robinson Sullivan
14.8.1. Eavie Mae Sullivan m. Grover Swor
14.8.2. Gettie Sullivan m. Shel Sullivan
14.8.3. Lafayette "Fatie" Sullivan (unmarried)
14.8.4. Neece Sullivan m. Bertha Sullivan
      1. Margie Sullivan m. Devoures Sullivan
        (children listed at 14.1.6.8)
      2. Geneva Sullivan m. Reed Tillman

3. Evie Mae Sullivan m. Donald Blakeney
4. Tom Sullivan m. Hazel Tanner
5. Bert Sullivan m. Claudie Ainsworth
6. Taylor Sullivan m. Ramona Young

14.8.5. Fairly Sullivan m. Eva Mae Craft

14.9 Wilson W. Sullivan m. Josephine Keyes
14.9.1. E. A. "Lon" Sullivan m. Edna Axton
14.9.2. Maetin Sullivan m. Alma Axton
14.9.3. Ina Sullivan m. Jerome Runnels
14.9.4. Edna Sullivan m. Robert Lerner
14.9.5. Gertha Sullivan m. Hines Hurley
14.9.6. Ethel Sullivan m. Homer Valentine
14.9.7. Robert "Bob" Sullivan m. Charity Little
14.9.8. Lola Sullivan m. Wallie Nelson
14.9.9. Virgil Sullivan (died)

14.10 Martha M. "Matt" Sullivan m. C. C. "Conn" Sullivan
14.10.1. Mamie Sullivan m. _____ Easterling
14.10.2. Della Sullivan m. "Bud" Sullivan
14.10.3. Delia Sullivan
14.10.4. Peter Sullivan
14.10.5. Pearcy Sullivan
14.10.6. Pearlie Sullivan
14.10.7. Searcy Sullivan
14.10.8. Broadus Sullivan
14.10.9. Beulah Sullivan

Selected Bibliography

BOOKS

Baker, Pearl R. *Neath Georgia Soil.* Albany, Ga.: Mary Carter Press, 1970.

Bettersworth, John K. *Mississippi: A History.* Austin: Steck Co., 1959.

Bryan, Mary G. *Passports Issued by Governors of Georgia, 1785–1820.* 2 vols. Washington: National Genealogical Society, 1962–1964.

Bryant, Pat, and Marion R. Hemperley. *English Crown Grants in Georgia, 1755–1775.* 7 vols. Atlanta: Department of Archives and History, 1972–1974.

Black, Patti Carr. *Mississippi Piney Woods.* Jackson: Mississippi Department of Archives and History, 1976.

Carter, Clarence E. *The Territory of Alabama 1817–1819.* Repr., New York: AMS Press, 1973.

Comings, Lydia Jane Newcomb, and Martha M. Albers. *A Brief History of Baldwin County.* Fairhope, Ala.: Baldwin County Historical Society, 1928.

Coulter, Ellis M., and A. B. Saye. *A List of Early Settlers of Georgia.* Athens: University of Georgia Press, 1967.

DAR Alabama. *Index to Alabama Wills.* Ann Arbor: Society, 1955.

Davis, Minnie Spell. *True Confederates of Mississippi.* Hattiesburg: Geiger Printing Company, 1965.

Delwyn Associates. *Substitutes for Georgia's Lost 1790 Census.* Albany: The Compilers, 1974.

Ervin, Sara Sullivan. *South Carolineans in the Revolution.* Baltimore: Genealogical Publishing Co., 1965.

Georgia Genealogical Society. *Index to the Headright and Bounty Grants in Georgia from 1756–1909.* Easley, S.C.: Southern Historical Press, 1970.

Hendrix, Mary. *Mississippi Court Records from the Files of the High Court of Errors and Appeals 1799–1859.* Jackson: Privately printed, 1950.

Governor and Council Warrants for Land in South Carolina, 1672–1711. Rev. by R. N. Olsberg. Columbia: University of South Carolina Press, 1973.

Holcomb, Gene (ed.). *Mississippi: A Guide to the Magnolia State, American Guide Series.* New York: The Viking Press, 1938. Repr., New York: Hastings House, 1946.

Huxford, Folks. *Pioneers of Wiregrass Georgia.* 6 vols. Homerville, Ga.: Privately printed, 1948–1971.

J. E. Oglethorpe Chapter. *Saint Paul's Parish in the Colony of Georgia, 1758–77.* Savannah: Daughter of American Colony, 1958.

King, Janie Estelle. *Mississippi Court Records 1799–1835.* Repr., Baltimore: Genealogical Publishing Co., 1969.

Lancour, Aldore Harold. *Passenger List of Ships Coming to North America, 1607–1825.* New York: Privately printed, 1937.

Lucas, Silas E. *1807 Land Lottery of Georgia.* Easley, S.C.: Southern Historical Press, 1968.

———. *Some Georgia County Records.* Easley, S.C.: Southern Historical Press, 1977.

McBee, May Wilson. *The Natchez Court Records, 1767–1805.* 2 vols. Ann Arbor: Edwards Brothers, Inc., 1953. Repr., Baltimore: Genealogical Publishing Co., 1967.

Moore, Caroline T. *Abstracts of the Wills, State of South Carolina, 1670–1800.* 4 vols. Charleston: Privately printed, 1960–1974.

Rowland, Dunbar. *History of Mississippi.* Chicago: S. J. Clarke Publishing Co., 1925.

Sullivan, Chester. *Sullivan's Hollow.* Jackson: University Press of Mississippi, 1978.

Sullivan, Milton, *The Sullivan Family: The William Dunklin Line.* Privately printed, 1961.

Wood, Virginia S., and R. V. Wood. *1805 Land Lottery of Georgia.* Belmont, Mass.: Greenwood Press, 1964.

Wynd, Frances. *They Were Here.* 8 vols. Albany, Ga.: Privately printed, 1965–.

ARTICLES IN JOURNALS AND MAGAZINES

Baker, Pearl R. "Cemetery Records, Columbia County, Ga." *Neath Georgia Sod,* I, 3–45.

"Camden County, Georgia Deed Records." *Georgia Genealogy Magazine,* VII (1963), 361.

"Columbia County, Georgia, Early Court Records." *Georgia Pioneers,* VIII, 93.

"Early Alabama Trails." *Alabama Genealogy Register,* V (1963), 21.

"1805 Tax List, Georgia, Columbia County." *Georgia Genealogy Magazine,* VIII (1971), 137.

"Georgia Colonial Deed Book DD." *Georgia Genealogy Magazine,* XII (April, 1964), 700.

Henderson, Harry, and Sam Shaw. "The Sullivans of Sullivan's Hollow." *Colliers,* CXV (March, 1947), 20–21.

"Marriages, Liberty County, Ga." *Georgia Genealogy Magazine*, II (1964), 687.

Sartor, William. "Sullivan's Hollow: Meanest Valley in America." *Life*, October 2, 1967, pp. 1–2.

"Simpson County, 1823, Births and Deaths." *Mississippi Genealogical Society*, XVI (1970), 11.

Street, W. B. "Feuding, Fussing, and Going Sullivan." *Mid-South Magazine*, January 2, 1966, pp. 4–5.

"Tales and Legends from the Hollow." *Mississippi Chronicle of the South*, October 25, 1975, pp. 1–4.

NEWSPAPERS

"Sullivan Home 100 Years Olds." *Jackson Daily Clarion Ledger*, December 31, 1937.

"Sullivan Ruled Famous Hollow with an Iron Hand," *Memphis Commercial Appeal*, June 8, 1930.

McIntire, Carl. "Sullivan's Hollow Original Log Home Still Sullivan." *Jackson Daily Clarion Ledger*, October 22, 1972, Sec. G 1.

Thompson, Ray M. "Horseback in Mississippi." *Gulfport-Biloxi Daily Herald*, November 9, 1960.

———. "Mississippi's Famous Feuding Sullivans." *Gulfport-Biloxi Daily Herald*, 1957.

Watts, James. "Fiery legends of Sullivan's Hollow Still Echo Throughout the South." *Jackson Daily News*, June 20, 1967.

Wheeler, Lonnie. "Sullivan's Hollow—Fighting Family Heritage." *Jackson Daily Clarion Ledger*, October 31, 1977, Sec. A 16.

MISCELLANEOUS WORKS

"Abstracts of Georgia Colonial Conveyance, Book C-1." Compiled from Surveyor–General Land Deeds by F. H. Beckemeyer. Atlanta: R. J. Taylor, Jr. Foundation.

Bishop, Grover, and Session Fant. "History of Sullivan's Hollow." Unpublished manuscript. Coded: 800—Sullivan's Hollow, MS, Smith County, FC. Jackson: Mississippi Department of Archives and History, 1938.

Howell, Virgil M. "Authentic History of Sullivan's Hollow." Unpublished manuscript dictated by Wild Bill Sullivan. Tifton, Ga.: Ann Howell Hammons, 1930.

State of Mississippi vs. W. C. Sullivan. Trial Transcript, Case #11368. Flora, Miss., Records Center, 1905.

"Survey of Records in Mississippi Courthouses." Unpublished manuscript. Jackson: Mississippi Genealogical Society, 1970.

United States of America. "Federal Census Schedules." Atlanta: Federal Records Center, 1790–1900.

United States Public Land Office. "Applications for Homestead Registration, M.T. 1805–1822, Fort Saint Stephens." Journal A, Book 49, I.

Montgomery: Department of Archives and History.
United States Public Land Office. "Credit Ledger, Huntsville, East of the Pearl River." Book 192. Montgomery: Department of Archives and History.

MICROFILM
"Personal Tax Rolls, 1834–1848. Smith County, Mississippi." Jackson: Department of Archives and History, Roll #360.
"Smith County Deed Book." Jackson: Department of Archives and History. No Roll #.
"Tract Book, 1833–1909. Chancery Clerk, Smith County, Mississippi." Jackson: Department of Archives and History.
United States of America. "Compiled Service Records of Confederate Soldiers, Mississippi." Jackson: Department of Archives and History, Roll #269.

Index

141